NEW SUPERVISORS IN TECHNICAL SERVICES

A Management
Guide Using
Checklists

EDITED BY EMILY BERGMAN AND ANDREA KAPPLER

Technical Services and Systems Committee

Systems and Services Section

Library Administration and Management Association,
a division of the American Library Association

Chicago 2007

While extensive effort has gone into ensuring the reliability of information appearing in this book, the publisher makes no warranty, express or implied, on the accuracy or reliability of the information, and does not assume and hereby disclaims any liability to any person for any loss or damage caused by errors or omissions in this publication.

The paper used in this publication meets the minimum requirements of American National Standard for Information Sciences—Permanence of Paper for Printed Library Materials, ANSI Z39.48-1992.♾

Library of Congress Cataloging-in-Publication Data
Cataloging-in-Publication Data is on file with the Library of Congress

ISBN-10: 0-8389-8413-4
ISBN-13: 978-0-8389-8413-0

Printed in the United States of America

11 10 09 08 07   5 4 3 2 1

TABLE OF CONTENTS

EMILY BERGMAN
Head of Collections and Technical Services
Occidental College

Often, successful frontline technical services staff become supervisors for the first time. The fact that you asked for or were willing to accept the responsibility that comes with taking on new duties, which involves learning new skills, is one thing that distinguishes you. Someone may have seen the spark of leadership in you; this is the spark you must start developing. A leader is someone whose judgment is respected because it is usually sound. Moving into a supervisory role is a tremendous change, not only in the job and responsibilities, but also your viewpoint.

Many new managers think that managing means doing what they always have done but with more power and control. Instead, you need to go from concentrating on one task to coordinating the efforts of others and to understanding what they do. Know that the daily reality of managerial life can often be pressured, hectic, and fragmented. You must learn to respond to the unending, confusing, and sometimes conflicting demands of subordinates, bosses, and peers. Learn also to understand the power dynamics of your department or the library and its impact on your unit, and actively manage these external relationships so as not to jeopardize your success.

Many first-time managers have a notion of management that may be limited to the concept of formal authority and issues of power. Management is as much a position of dependence as authority. You supervise the people in your unit; you do not own them.

Listening with an open mind is one of the most important traits a new manager can demonstrate. Being able to delegate tasks to other staff members is vital to the success of a manager, which is not always easy after having done the work yourself. However, show your staff you do not expect them to do anything that you yourself would be unwilling to do. Learn to balance the paradoxical tensions in managing people, such as treating subordinates fairly and as individuals, holding them accountable yet tolerating their mistakes and deficiencies, and maintaining control while also providing autonomy. To treat people fairly is to treat each one differently, because the right amount of supervision or delegation for one person may be inappropriate for another. Along the way you will discover the trick of managing individuals while also providing leadership.

As you take on your new supervisory responsibility is a good time to learn what the individuals in the unit think about the operation, their own jobs, and what improvements they might suggest. Ask questions about policies and procedures but also the history and folklore. Do not push an agenda at the beginning; listen, learn, and evaluate how your ideas will mesh with the people and the organization of your new unit and the rest of the library. Through your encouragement of the staff's participation in planning and decision-making, a group of people will develop on whom you can count to help you help them achieve, both personally and as a unit. A supervisor also needs to be able to plan and coordinate, manage time, and make decisions. Finally, new managers should remember the intangible qualities like self-confidence, flexibility, creativity, and a sense of humor.

One concern in beginning a supervisory assignment is learning the details of the job as quickly as possible. Though the natural inclination may be to think that learning the job will take forever, what is unfamiliar may appear more difficult than it actually is. Using the checklists in this book is one way to help you through the learning process. Almost all the problems you encounter may be new to you, but many other supervisors have experienced them. Use that experience to help you. Some organizations may practice the "sink or swim" theory of management training. Not everyone knows what to do or how to do it, so use the checklists to help keep your head above water as you move through the various responsibilities as a new manager. Be aware of the skills you lack before a problem arises. Improve as a manager by collecting feedback, analyzing it, and altering behavior as necessary.

These checklists are for all first-time supervisors in technical services. Those who work in library technical services often get placed in supervisory positions without any preparation. A periodicals assistant may supervise clerks or student assistants and be responsible for the whole periodicals unit; a cataloger may become head cataloger, supervising librarians, library assistants, and perhaps other units such as preparation and bindery; or the acquisitions librarian may be promoted to head of technical services and have responsibility for several units and several layers of employees. This manual is meant for anyone in a supervisory capacity in technical services, both librarians and library assistants; in any type or size of library; and in any area of responsibility. It is to be kept with you, used, and written in. It is practical, not theoretical. Selected bibliographies are included at the end of each section for further reading; there is also a lot of very good literature out there for library workers to glean. Of course, the contributors to this book hope it continues to be of use to supervisors who are no longer in their first-time supervisory position as well as be an aid to middle- and upper-level managers mentoring new supervisors.

The members of the Technical Services and Systems Committee (TSSC) of the Systems and Services Section of the Library Administration and Management Association contributed all the sections during a four-year period. The individual authors are listed within each section, and I would like to thank each of them for their insight and writing to make this as useful as possible for all first-time supervisors, as well as my coeditor Andrea Kappler for her dedicated work. Mostly, I would like to thank Randy Call, who chaired TSSC and not only proposed the publication, but created the structure and began the process of generating the subject areas for the various sections and how they fit into the chapters.

BIBLIOGRAPHY

Belker, Loren B., and Gary S. Topchik. *The First-Time Manager.* New York: AMACOM, 2005.

Giesecke, Joan., ed. *Practical Help for New Supervisors.* Chicago: ALA, 1997.

Hill, Linda A. "Hardest Lessons for First-Time Managers." *Working Woman* 19 (Feb. 1994): 18–21.

Piccininni, James. "Advice for First-time Library Directors on Managing a Library." *Library Administration & Management* 10, no. 1 (Winter 1996): 41–43.

Sopwards, Steven W. "Observations of a First-Year Middle Manager: Thirteen Tips That Can Save You." *College & Research Libraries News* 60, no. 7 (Jul./Aug. 1999): 523–25.

PLANNING

Creating Mission, Goals, and Objectives

MICHELLE R. TURVEY
Original Cataloger
Kansas State University Libraries

There is no shortage of advice when it comes to writing a mission statement, setting goals, and creating objectives. The business literature is literally overflowing. Numerous books, articles, and Web sites are devoted to writing mission statements.

A mission statement should state succinctly the reason for your department's existence. Experts suggest editing if the statement is would not fit on a tee shirt, coffee mug, or business card. Writing a mission statement forces you to conduct some basic strategic planning. Done correctly, mission statements can unify a department and foster a shared vision. Mission statements can also serve as a tool to guide decision-making.

According to Wallace, a mission statement should: establish focus, identify your stakeholders and how they are served, encourage staff and donors, and create a means of measuring effectiveness.[1] Consider breaking the mission statement down into a smaller series of questions that ask who, what, for whom, and why the organization or department does what it does.

Be aware of the difference between a vision statement and a mission statement. A vision statement sets the long-term direction. The vision statement is where you want to be in the future. In contrast, the mission statement focuses on the immediate and the short-term.

I. **Mission statements**
    A. Qualities of a good mission statement
        ____ The statement addresses its target audience (The target audience for technical services may differ slightly from the library in general.)
        ____ The statement is broadly written (not a laundry list of what the department does)
        ____ The statement uses an active voice

---

1. Linda K. Wallace, *Libraries, Mission & Marketing: Writing Mission Statements That Work* (Chicago: ALA, 2004).

_____ The statement is memorable and easy for the public and the employees to recall

_____ The statement is short and succinct

_____ The writing style is clear and jargon-free so that others outside of technical services can readily understand it

_____ It details what your department accomplishes for the library

_____ It is reviewed and revised on a regular basis

_____ The department mission statement ties into the library's mission statement

_____ The department mission statement ties back into the library's values and goals

_____ The statement is compelling and inspiring

B. What to avoid in a mission statement

_____ The statement is filled with out-of-date terminology

_____ The text is clichéd and unoriginal

_____ The statement uses a one-size-fits-all approach rather than one tailored to your department and library

II. Goals

_____ The goals transform the mission into action

_____ The goals are concrete

_____ The goals are tangible

_____ The goals are measurable

_____ Each goal has an assigned priority

_____ The performance goals tie directly to the mission statement

_____ The goals are realistic

III. Objectives

_____ The objectives provide concrete means of reaching your department's goals

_____ The objectives provide deadlines

_____ The objectives are linked closely to the department's goals and aligned with the mission statement

_____ The objectives are SMART (Specific, Measurable, Achievable, Relevant, and Time-bound)[2]

SELECTED BIBLIOGRAPHY

Abrahams, Jeffrey. *The Mission Statement Book: 301 Corporate Mission Statements from America's Top Companies.* Rev. ed. Berkeley, Calif.: Ten Speed Pr., 1999.

Charney, Cy. *The Instant Manager: More Than 100 Quick Tips and Techniques for Great Results.* Rev. ed. New York: AMACOM, 2004.

Giesecke, Joan and Beth McNeil. *Fundamentals of Library Supervision.* Chicago: ALA, 2005.

Hartzell, Gary. "Controlling Your Own Destiny: Why Vision and Mission Statements Are Indispensable." *School Library Journal* 48, no. 11 (Nov. 2002): 37.

Hartzell, Gary. "Promises You Can't Keep: There's Only So Much a Librarian Can Realistically Accomplish." *School Library Journal* 48, no. 12 (Dec. 2002): 31.

Peter F. Drucker Foundation for Nonprofit Management. "Drucker Foundation Self-Assessment Tool: Content. How to Develop a Mission Statement," *The Drucker Foundation Self-Assessment Tool: Process Guide.* San Francisco, Calif.: Jossey-Bass, 1999. Reprinted by the Leader to Leader Institute at www.leadertoleader.org/knowledgecenter/sat/mission.html (accessed Jan. 23, 2007).

2. Joan Giesecke and Beth McNeil, *Fundamentals of Library Supervision* (Chicago: ALA, 2005).

Senge, Peter M. "The Discipline of Innovation." *Executive Excellence* 16, no. 6 (Jun. 1999): 10–11.

Vogt, Jean. "Demystifying the Mission Statement." *Nonprofit World* 12, no. 1 (Jan./Feb. 1994): 29–32.

Wall, Bob, Robert S. Solum, and Mark R. Sobol. *The Mission-Driven Organization: From Mission Statement to a Thriving Enterprise, Here's Your Blueprint for Building an Inspired, Cohesive Customer-Oriented Team.* Rocklin, Calif.: Prima Pub., 1999.

Wallace, Linda K. *Libraries, Mission & Marketing: Writing Mission Statements That Work.* Chicago: ALA, 2004.

Notes

Budgeting

SHARON CASTLEBERRY
Systems Librarian
DeSoto Public Library

NANCY LEE MYERS
Acquisitions Librarian and Professor
University of South Dakota

The budget defines the operational possibilities for the library during a given period of time. It defines the health of the organization and its ability to provide services to a growing, increasingly diverse population that is demanding a greater variety of library materials in many formats. Budgeting for library services is one of a manager's most important tasks. During booming economic times, you may find it easy to justify an increasing budget to the library's governing body, but in times of gloomy financial forecasts, library services may be seen by that same body as nonessential.

Budget documents generally need to adhere to a format specified by the parent organization. There are several different types of budgets: line item budgets, program budgets, zero-based budgets, performance budgets, and five-year or long-range budgets. An organization may choose to use any of these types of budgeting procedures. To compile a budget, you need to have a good understanding and knowledge of the library's expenses, sources of revenue, and plans for future growth. Timelines are generally given in which current budget expenditures and revenues should be estimated. Future budgets are based upon costing forecasts derived from the current budget estimates. You need to be able to understand fully and produce a comprehensive budget as a plan for current, future and long-range library growth.

I. **Budget history**
    Examine budget statements and end-of-year statements for the last three years to get the history of the organization and determine trends.
    A. Expenses
        ____ Personnel (salaries and fringe benefits)
        ____ Postage
        ____ Library materials (books; periodicals; electronic databases; and audiovisual resources such as videos, DVDs, and CDs)
        ____ Processing or outsourcing costs
        ____ Travel (conference attendance and continuing education)
        ____ Interlibrary loan and document delivery
        ____ Equipment

_____ Computers (hardware and software)
_____ Copiers
_____ Fax machines
_____ Microform readers and printers
_____ Scanners
_____ Storage (stacks or storage units for books, periodicals, microfilm, CDs, videos, DVDs, etc.)
_____ Maintenance (cleaning, repairs)
_____ Prepayments
_____ Payment schedules
_____ Nonrecurring expenses
_____ Integrated library system
_____ Contingency

B. Sources of income
_____ Allocation or formula budget from governing body (city, state, federal government, parent organization, etc.)
_____ Grants
_____ Consortial arrangements

II. Current budget
_____ Examine the current budget and present allocation of resources
_____ Plan for any necessary or desirable changes for the current fiscal year, providing changes are possible
_____ Arrange for automatically generated monthly reports for monitoring purposes

III. Budget planning
_____ Make recommendations to the governing body for the next fiscal year
_____ Utilize cost projections to estimate expenses
_____ Determine new plans and needs for the next fiscal year based on the library's mission and goals
_____ New staff needed to support new programs and initiatives (professional and support staff)
_____ Professional development requirements for new staff
_____ New technology and equipment needed for new programs and new staff
_____ New service agreements for new equipment
_____ Increase in utility or maintenance needs
_____ Increase in library materials needed to support new programs or collections
_____ New electronic resources needed to support new programs or collections
_____ New programs to be implemented (supplies, consultant expenses, etc.)
_____ Formulate base budget to account for current levels of service for new fiscal year
_____ Prepare long-range (three-to-five year) financial plans, based on your library's mission statement and goals

A. Staffing
_____ Raises (determined by the Consumer Price Index)
_____ Benefits based upon new salaries
_____ Benefits based on a flat rate

B. Supplies
_____ Include percentage price increases determined by trend analysis
_____ Determine if the current number of supplies will still be needed or if more processing and packaging should be outsourced

C. Professional development
   ____ Travel expenses for professional staff (required for promotion and retention)
   ____ Training expenses for line and professional staff
   ____ Membership dues
   ____ Mileage reimbursements
D. Services (forecast on trend analysis or known price increases)
   ____ Forecast increases in maintenance and utilities
   ____ Forecast increase in telecommunications
   ____ Forecast increase in postage
   ____ Forecast increase in printing
E. Library materials
   ____ Determine any increases in serials based on published information or from serials jobbers
   ____ Determine any increases in print materials from published information
   ____ Determine any increases in electronic materials by calling vendors
   ____ Add desired capital items to base budget
      ____ Computer equipment
      ____ Furniture and fixtures
      ____ Building additions
      ____ Office equipment

SELECTED BIBLIOGRAPHY

German, Lisa, and Nancy Slight-Gibney, eds. *Guide to the Management of the Information Resources Budget.* New York: Scarecrow Pr., 2001.

Giesecke, Joan. *Practical Strategies for Library Managers.* Chicago: ALA, 2001.

Koenig, Michael, ed. *Budgeting Techniques for Libraries and Information Centers.* Professional Development Series, vol. 1. New York: Special Libraries Association, 1980.

Martin, Murray S., and Sheila S. Intner, eds. *Collection Development and Finance: A Guide to Strategic Library-Materials Budgeting.* Frontiers of Access to Library Materials, no. 2. Chicago: ALA, 1995.

Martin, Murray S., and Milton T. Wolf. *Budgeting for Information Access: Managing the Resource Budget for Absolute Access.* Frontiers of Access to Library Materials, no. 4. Chicago: ALA, 1998.

Shreeves, Edward, ed. *Guide to Budget Allocation for Information Resources.* Collection Management and Development Guides, no. 4. Chicago: ALA, 1991.

Taft Group Staff. *The Big Book of Library Grant Money 2006: Profiles of Private and Corporate Foundations and Direct Corporate Givers Receptive to Library Grant Proposals.* Chicago: ALA, 2006.

Warner, Alice S. *Budgeting: A How-to-Do-It Manual for Librarians.* New York: Neal-Schuman, 1998.

Notes

Planning for Technology

ANDREA KAPPLER
Cataloging Manager
Evansville Vanderburgh Public Library

Planning for technology in technical services departments requires that you have knowledge of both computer hardware and software, in addition to being aware of overall trends in computer technology and in libraries, particularly as they relate to units within technical services. In the past, computers changed so slowly that a library could use older hardware and software for many years before needing to upgrade. But with the advent of the Internet and new forms of software—and their vital use as library tools—you are faced with making technical decisions that did not exist a decade ago.

Quite often, new software drives the need to upgrade hardware, as programs become more complex and require more computing power. The move away from printed documentation also presents both training and management issues that were nonexistent a decade ago. Changes in technology present ongoing training challenges, as your staff will need continual training in addition to their educational backgrounds. As a manager, you will need to provide this training, often at little or no expense to your department, to keep your staff current as new cataloging technologies arise.

I. **Hardware**
    A. Computers, monitors, keyboards, and mice
        ____ Know minimum hardware requirements for both library and non-library vendors, such as Microsoft
        ____ Work with the administration to make sure the budget enables technical services staff to have computers replaced or upgraded every two to three years
        ____ Make sure staff workstations are ergonomically designed and efficient
        ____ Replace faulty or failing equipment as soon as possible
        ____ Know whom to contact in your organization to report problems with hardware
        ____ Keep current with technology changes by reading computer industry publications
    B. Printers and scanners
        ____ Know the difference between dot matrix, laser, and inkjet printers and how to use them
        ____ Decide whether staff have their own printers or share networked printers
        ____ Know the difference between flatbed and sheetfeeder scanners and how to use them

_____ Replace faulty or failing printers and scanners as soon as possible

C. Barcode readers

_____ Know the difference between light pens, handheld scanners, and portable barcode readers and how to use them

_____ Replace faulty or failing barcode readers as soon as possible

II. Software

A. Integrated Library System (ILS)

_____ Work with the administration to budget for new products and upgrades to the ILS

_____ Attend ILS user group meetings and national library conferences to keep up with new products, pricing, and changes to ILS software

_____ Maintain communication with the ILS vendor to make sure it is keeping up with changes in cataloging formats, such as MARC format, Dublin Core, etc.

_____ Maintain communication with the ILS vendor to make sure it is keeping up with handling new formats, such as electronic materials and digital images

_____ Make sure new releases of software are loaded on schedule and the library does not fall behind the vendors' recommended release installation schedules for their software

_____ Budget for and request training from the ILS vendor if its software changes radically or new modules are purchased

_____ Know whom to contact in your organization to report problems with ILS software

B. PC operating systems

_____ Know the difference between the Microsoft operating system and others, as well as latest versions supported by manufacturers

_____ Budget for upgrades to PC operating systems every two to three years

_____ Make sure the operating system is compatible with the ILS and make upgrades when necessary to maintain compatibility with the ILS software

_____ Know whether the PC operating systems are on a network or on individual PCs

_____ Make sure staff are trained to use the operating system, especially if it is part of a network

_____ Know whom to contact in your organization to report problems with PC software

C. Networks

_____ Have a basic working knowledge of networked software and equipment in technical services and how it is linked to the larger organization

_____ Be aware of computer networks outside of your organization to which you may belong now or in the future

_____ Know whom to contact in your organization to report problems with networked equipment

D. Software for technical services workstations

_____ Be aware of software from ILS vendors or other vendors that streamlines basic Technical Services operations such as collection development (e.g., Titletales, TitleSource, iPage, GOBI), acquisitions software (e.g., electronic ordering or invoicing), serials software (e.g., electronic invoicing and claiming) and binding software (e.g., ABLE, SF-Systems, LINCPlus, Aleph)

_____ Cataloging software

_____ Be aware of the different vendors of bibliographic and authority records and know what hardware and software is required to access their databases

_____ Budget for the data supplied by bibliographic and authority vendors

_____ Install updates as recommended by bibliographic and authority vendors

_____ Know which vendors offer products on CD-ROM or as Web services

        1. CD-ROMs
- ____ Know which vendors offer their products in CD-ROM format
- ____ Budget for CD-ROM products and licensing fees
- ____ Know which CD-ROM products can be loaded onto network servers or individual PCs
- ____ Budget time and money for staff training

        2. Web services
- ____ Know which services are provided free by vendors and individuals
- ____ Know which vendors provide services requiring subscription and licensing fees
- ____ Budget for Web subscription and licensing fees
- ____ Obtain necessary permissions and passwords
- ____ Budget time and money for staff training

____ Technical services Internet and Intranet pages
- ____ Know who designs and maintains departmental pages
- ____ Make sure departmental documentation and Web links are kept up-to-date

____ Know whom to contact to report problems with bibliographic and authority vendors, their CD-ROM products or Web services, and local Internet and Intranet pages

E. Miscellaneous standards and software

____ Know MARC bibliographic and authority formats and be aware of how they are loaded and indexed in your local system

____ Keep current with changes in cataloging formats and standards, such as AACR2R, RDA, MARC, Dublin Core, and others

____ Familiarize yourself with the Z39.50 communications protocol and investigate whether or not it can be used with your local system and other library vendors

____ Learn how to use FTP to send and receive files to and from vendors

____ Provide e-mail software and accounts for staff to monitor discussion lists, communicate with public services staff, and maintain communications within technical services

____ Provide virus protection software and train staff to update this software on their PCs

____ Be able to use and make sure staff is able to use PC software, such as word processing, spreadsheets, and databases

____ Work with public services staff in implementation of new ILS modules, if there are major changes to public modules (i.e., OPAC), or if the library is seeking a new automation vendor

III. Staff training and documentation

____ Know the educational levels of technical services staff

____ Decide whether staff need in-house training, Web training, a visit from a trainer, or offsite training

____ Budget for training every year

____ Provide follow-up or retraining if necessary

____ Make sure training materials are available for referral after training is completed

SELECTED BIBLIOGRAPHY

Gorman, Michael. *Technical Services Today and Tomorrow.* Englewood, Colo.: Libraries Unlimited, 1998.

Kaplan, Michael, ed. *Planning and Implementing Technical Services Workstations.* Chicago: ALA, 1997.

Notes

Emergency Preparedness

JUNE DEWEESE
Head of Access Services Division
University of Missouri-Columbia

MARLENE SLOUGH
Head of Acquisitions
Eastern Illinois University

Adisaster is a natural or person-made occurrence that threatens human safety and causes damage to library facilities and materials. A disaster can be minor: a window left open during a sudden thunderstorm, a window well that gets clogged with leaves and overflows, or a water pipe breaking. Or it can be major: a flood, a massive fire, a tornado, or an act of terrorism. The basic principle of emergency preparedness is to plan for a disaster you hope never will occur. A written document should be available both in paper and on the library's Web site. The document should be reviewed and updated at least annually. It should be discussed at any new staff orientation program the library uses, as well as in periodic refresher sessions for long-term staff.

Technical services librarians and staff will be involved in any disaster response and recovery efforts because of their day-to-day responsibilities and expertise. They will work closely and collaboratively with other library staff and emergency response persons from outside the library. If the preservation department is a part of technical services, it will be very involved in each aspect of the work and play a critical role in salvage and recovery in any disaster, large or small.

Consider having a disaster plan for technical services based on the library's plan or as a section of the larger plan. Include issues that are specific to technical services—for example, materials and equipment may be more important than people, since there are no library patrons in the department.

I. **Create a disaster preparedness manual**
    ____ Write a manual that outlines step-by-step instructions to be followed in the case of different types of disasters. It should be specific to your library
    ____ Work with public services, access or circulation services, library administration, and other stakeholders in the library to determine what needs to be included in the manual

  A. Establish a disaster response team
    A disaster response team is the group of people who will be first on the scene of any disaster and will make initial evaluations and contacts and determine what needs to be done first
    ____ Convene a meeting to determine who would be the best representatives

_____ Consult with other division heads or administrators to determine whom they are appointing and what criteria they use to make the appointments

_____ Determine with those division heads what expertise is needed and use that information when choosing a representative from technical services

_____ Include in the meeting the most appropriate persons in technical services to provide input and help you make the best decision

_____ Determine the technical services representatives to the team

_____ Make and keep up-to-date a list of all persons on the team including home and cell phone numbers

_____ Each team member should keep a copy of that list at home, at work, and in another place, such as the glove compartment of the vehicle that the person generally drives

_____ Establish a procedure for notifying each team member

_____ Establish a procedure for notifying library administration and others who need to know about a disaster, even though they may not be on the disaster response team

B. Determine a series of meeting places for the disaster response team to gather, depending upon each type of disaster and the location of the problem

_____ Each person responding to a disaster should know the locations of the meeting places and go there to gather with other library staff, institutional and community law enforcement, and other emergency responders

_____ Each person should have a list of equipment and supplies to bring personally, in addition to those items that they can reasonably expect to find for their use at the meeting places

_____ Flashlight

_____ Cell phone

_____ Hardhat

_____ Rain gear

C. Establish a salvage team and determine salvage priorities for each library. In smaller libraries, the salvage team and the disaster response team may be the same persons. In larger libraries, the composition of these teams should be different to maximize the talents and expertise of each team member as well as to divide the workload. The salvage team may be mostly technical services staff

_____ Have floor plans for each library showing each stack and work area

_____ Determine the process for recovery and salvage

_____ Determine which person will do which task

_____ Determine the process for salvage of paper-based materials

_____ Determine the process for salvage of nonpaper materials

_____ Microformat materials

_____ Sound recordings

_____ Visual materials

_____ Photographic materials

_____ Other nonpaper format materials (define these for each library)

_____ Equipment, computers, and other resources

_____ Determine what work can be done on site or locally

_____ Have a predetermined location for freeze-drying wet materials and a plan to get materials to that location

_____ Have a damage assessment form that is easy to use and is in checklist format

II. **Evacuation plans**

_____ Create one for each building

_____ Have an evacuation plan for quickly exiting the building

    ____ Fire
    ____ Act of nature (i.e., earthquake, tornado, hurricane)
    ____ Acts of terrorism
    ____ Chemical spill
    ____ Bomb threats and bomb realities

____ Include egress through all of the exits available, even those not generally used
____ Allow for some of those exits being unavailable because of the disaster
____ Be prepared to help identify and clear the building of all library users
____ Have natural disaster evacuation plans in place so that people know where safe areas are in each building away from doors, windows and upper floors. Plans will differ depending upon the type of condition—tornado, earthquake, flood, etc.

III. Have plans in place to deal with aberrant activity

____ Terrorism
____ Vandalism
____ Bomb threats and bomb realities
____ Chemical-induced crises
____ Other threats to the safety and security of library employees and patrons

IV. Have a communication plan in place to use to communicate with:

____ Library employees
____ Library patrons
____ The media
____ Members of the community who need information about library services during the disaster recovery phase

V. Conduct regular drills to

____ Determine if everyone understands the written plans
____ Determine if everyone can put them into action if needed

VI. Considerations for technical services

____ Be prepared to take the lead in salvage
____ Determine what library materials to rescue
____ Decide what should be done in the technical services department
    ____ Materials
    ____ Equipment
    ____ Library's integrated library system
        ____ Computers
        ____ Databases
        ____ Back ups

HELPFUL WEB SITES

These Web sites offer templates for disaster plans:
- http://ieldrn.org/sample.htm (accessed Apr. 17, 2007)
- www.nedcc.org/plam3/index3.htm (accessed Apr. 17, 2007)
- www.dplan.org (accessed Apr. 17, 2007)

The following Web sites also provide a great deal of information for anyone working in emergency preparedness.

Conservation OnLine (CoOL) at Stanford University is a "full text library of conservation information, covering a wide spectrum of topics of interest to those involved with the conservation of library, archives and museum materials." (From the first page of the Web site), http://palimpsest.stanford.edu (accessed Apr. 17, 2007)

The **Association of College and Research Libraries** has a Web page on disaster preparedness: www .ala.org/ala/acrl/acrlpubs/crlnews/backissues2002/novmonth/crisisdisaster.htm (accessed Apr. 17, 2007)

SELECTED BIBLIOGRAPHY

Breighner, Mary, and William Payton. *Risk and Insurance Management Manual for Libraries.* Chicago: Library Administration and Management Association, 2005.

Kahn, Miriam. *Disaster Response and Planning for Libraries.* Chicago: ALA, 2003.

Successful Working Relationships with Procurement Departments

JUNE DEWEESE
Head of Access Services Division
University of Missouri–Columbia

ANDREA KAPPLER
Cataloging Manager
Evansville Vanderburgh Public Library

Technical services librarians and staff in most types of libraries work with procurement, purchasing, or business departments to purchase items meeting certain criteria, including a general price range. The nature of library resources and their purchase sometimes are not well understood by purchasing or procurement officers. Build a good collegial working relationship as soon as possible, and keep the lines of communication open to answer questions that they may have.

The first thing you need to do is find out the specific rules and regulations that govern the procurement process in your institution. The bid process is one that is frequently followed, especially with resources that cost more than a specified amount. You should ask for your institution's definition of a *sole source* bid. This is very important information, because many orders for books, databases, and the like often constitute a sole source bid. The ideal solution is to negotiate an exemption from standard procurement rules for library materials purchases.

Another key item involves Requests for Proposals (RFPs) for large contracts, such as approval plans, journal subscription packages, and contracts for the binding of materials. The requirements for RFPs are often quite specific and are based upon a set of specifications that may seem totally unrelated to library resources. During a bid process, you should adhere to all institutional rules regarding contact with vendors involved in the process, including those governing the acceptance of gifts.

I. **Procurement officers**
   _____ Find out if procurement officers are assigned based upon divisions of the city or academic institution (e.g., library)
   _____ Find out if procurement officers are assigned based upon types of items being procured and if they work with all divisions (e.g., couriers, equipment, furniture, print resources)

II. **Procedures and requirements**
   _____ Ask if there are general forms that must be filled out each time a request is sent to procurement

_____ Find out if there are price limits that require a bidding process
_____ Find out if there are criteria other than price that require a bidding process. (If so, what are they?)
_____ Find out if there are requirements for in-state vendors to be considered first in all purchases
     _____ Ask if there are any exceptions
     _____ Find out what paperwork is required to file for an exception
_____ Find out the general timeline involved after one submits a RFP to procurement
     _____ Ask if there is a fast track option available for rush items
     _____ If there is a fast track option, find out how you request it

III. RFP process

_____ Find out what role you can have in the RFP process
     _____ Can you write the RFP document?
     _____ Can you participate in the opening of the bids?
     _____ Can you request that the lowest bidder not be accepted; if so, under what conditions?
_____ Find out if there are prohibitions regarding interaction with vendors during the RFP process
     _____ Phone calls
     _____ Fax
     _____ E-mail
_____ Find out the institutional regulations regarding acceptance of gifts from vendors
     _____ Price
     _____ Timing
     _____ Type
     _____ Paperwork involved to record

IV. Sole source bids

_____ Find out if your institution permits sole source bids
_____ If they are permitted, find out what the rules are for using a sole source bid and when one is justified instead of the competitive bidding process
_____ Find out what information is needed to justify a sole source bid and start a file of documentation that applies to various types of purchases
     _____ Monographs (books)
     _____ Journals
     _____ Electronic resources
     _____ Library binding
     _____ Other resources

V. Documentation

_____ Find out if your procurement or purchasing department has written documentation outlining all of the rules and regulations of your institution that can be shared with you
_____ If there is general documentation, find out if you can work with someone in the procurement or purchasing department to edit the documentation specifically for unique purchases relating to the library
_____ If there is no documentation, find out if you can work with someone in the procurement or purchasing department to write pertinent documentation that both departments may use to make the process most efficient in the future

SELECTED BIBLIOGRAPHY

Couts, Mona C., Charles L. Gilreath, Joe A. Hewitt, and John Ulmschneider. "Use of a General Concept Paper as RFP for a Library System: A New Model for Library System Procurement." *Advances in Library Automation and Networking* 5 (1994): 177–202.

Flowers, Janet. "Negotiations with Library Materials Vendors: Preparation and Tips." *The Bottom Line* 16, no. 3 (2003): 100–106.

Holt, Glen E. "Buyer-Seller Relationships: How Libraries Can Make the System Work." *The Bottom Line* 17, no. 2 (2004): 66.

Stern, David. "Pricing Models and Payment Schemes for Library Collections." *Online* 26, no. 5 (Sept./Oct. 2002): 54–60.

ACKNOWLEDGEMENT

June DeWeese acknowledges the invaluable assistance of her colleague and friend, Alice J. Allen, associate director of technical services, University of Missouri–Columbia, who provided a great deal of advice regarding the content of June's portion of this article.

Notes

Measuring Productivity

MARLENE SLOUGH
Head of Acquisitions
Eastern Illinois University

We live in a culture of assessment and increasing accountability. Performance assessment, whether continuous or periodic, is a practice that has permeated public, academic, school, and special libraries alike. Performance measurement in libraries has been traditionally qualitative in nature. It is primarily a management tool. Knowledge gained through a systematic process of assessment can assist you in identifying best practices and lead to more effective and efficient operating procedures. Improving both the quality and the quantity of library resources and services is the ultimate reason to measure productivity.

I. **Applications of productivity measurements**

_____ To satisfy reporting requests (e.g., administration, organization, consortia, government)

_____ To support budget requests (e.g., salaries, collections, equipment, and supplies)

_____ To allocate or reallocate existing resources (e.g., salaries, collections, equipment, supplies, and staff)

_____ To evaluate workflow, unit operations, and procedures

_____ To assist management in planning

_____ To assist in effective resource use and continuous improvement efforts

_____ To strengthen accountability

II. **Methods and models**

_____ Best practices

_____ Internal client user surveys

_____ Benchmarking

_____ Software packages (e.g., OCLC)

_____ Association of Research Libraries initiatives (e.g., LibQual+)

_____ American Library Association standards (e.g., PLA, ACRL)

_____ National standards (e.g, Integrated Postsecondary Education Data System [IPEDS])

_____ International standards (e.g., International Federation of Library Associations [IFLA] and International Organization for Standardization [ISO])

III. **Measurement considerations**

_____ Validity (the measurement measures what it is intended to measure)

_____ Reliability (the data is collected consistently and accurately)

_____ Responsiveness (the measurements reflect changes in procedures, workflows, resources, and services)

_____ The current measurement system may not be perfect, so be receptive to change

IV. **Technical services productivity measures**

A. Staff

_____ Number of tasks completed

_____ Number of errors

_____ Types of errors

_____ Group productivity

_____ Individual productivity

_____ Time to complete a function (order, invoice, claim, classify, index, physically prepare, holdings registration, declassify, etc.)

B. Vendors

_____ Usage statistics

_____ Content stability

_____ Content accuracy

_____ Accessibility to content

_____ Accessibility to technical support

_____ Update schedule

_____ Error rate

_____ Value added by the service or product

_____ Expenditures

_____ Efficiency (fill rate, errors, cancellations, and timeliness)

C. Department processes and workflows

_____ Number processed by format

_____ Number processed by classification

_____ Number of volumes processed

_____ Number of units processed

_____ Number of supplies utilized

_____ Number received by method of delivery

_____ Expenditures by format

_____ Expenditures by classification

_____ Number by physical space requirements (shelving needs)

_____ Number by special treatment requirements

SELECTED BIBLIOGRAPHY

ALCTS Serials Section Acquisitions Committee. "Guide to Performance Evaluation of Serials Vendors." *Managing Information* 5, no. 3 (Mar. 1998): 47.

Alsbury, Donna. "Looking Beyond Service Charge: Performance Evaluation of Serials Vendors: A Report of the Program Presented by the ALCTS Serials Section Acquisitions Committee." *Technical Services Quarterly* 13, no. 3/4 (1996): 115–17.

Bazirjian, Rosann, and Nancy M. Stanley. "Assessing the Effectiveness of Team-based Structures in Libraries." *Library Collections, Acquisitions, and Technical Services* 25, no. 2 (Summer 2001): 131–57.

Brown, Lynne Branche. "Evaluating the Outsourcing of Technical Services: How Do You Know If You're There If You Don't Know Where You're Going? A Report of the ALCTS Commercial Technical Services Committee Program." *Technical Services Quarterly* 18, no. 4 (2001): 58–62.

Burek, Ann. "One Person's View of Supervising Paraprofessionals." *Colorado Libraries* 26, no. 1 (Spring 2000): 25–26.

Dole, Wanda V., and Sherry S. Chang. "Consortium Use of the OCLC/AMIGOS Collection Analysis CD: The SUNY Experience." *Library Resources and Technical Services* 41, no. 1 (Jan. 1997): 50–57.

Johansson, David H. "On Overview of Collecting, Using, and Reporting Output Statistics in a Technical Services Department." *Public Library Quarterly* 16, no. 3 (1997): 25–41.

Lingle, Virginia A. "Selecting Processes to Bench-mark: A Key Step to Quality Improvement." *Health Libraries Review* 12, no. 3 (Sept. 1995): 218–21.

Zuidema, Karen Huwald. "Reengineering Technical Services Processes." *Library Resources and Technical Services* 43, no. 1 (Jan. 1999): 37–52.

Notes

Continuing Education

EMILY BERGMAN
Head of Collections and Technical Services
Occidental College

MELORA RANNEY NORMAN
Outreach/Special Services Coordinator
Maine State Library

Good managers have long known that continuing education plays an important role in job satisfaction and the retention of employees. An institution will find that in the long term, allowing employees the challenges and opportunities for advancement created by ongoing learning is in everyone's best interest. As a supervisor, you will need to gather information from the field and share it with your employees to create opportunities for discussion, innovation, creativity, and improvements in the workplace, as well as to keep pace with current developments and technological trends.

Timid employees gain confidence through positive peer instruction experiences. Ambitious, extroverted staff find job satisfaction if their positions entail ongoing options for advancement within their present positions; hence, they will stay longer and work better with a new understanding of their chosen field.

A good continuing education program for your employees will include a good balance of onsite peer activities, local options, and a reasonable number of opportunities for traveling to major conferences, events, and workshops to provide networking and broad perspective on the profession.

I. **Continuing education goals (there may be more than one of the following)**
    _____ Keeping up with new knowledge relating to the profession
    _____ Establishing mastery of new concepts
    _____ Continuing the study of basic disciplines that support the profession
    _____ Growing as a person as well as a professional

II. **Recipients of continuing education**
    _____ Supervisor
    _____ Staff

III. **Reasons for continuing education**
    _____ New job
    _____ New position
    _____ New technology
    _____ Advancement

    ____ Continuing education credits
    ____ Preparation to be promoted
    ____ Morale

IV. Continuing education sources
  A. Out-of-library
    ____ Professional institutes
    ____ Enrollment in courses at local universities
    ____ Participation in conferences and workshops
    ____ Job exchanges
  B. In-house
    ____ Apprenticeship
    ____ Contract training
    ____ Staff as trainer
    ____ Reports from conferences
    ____ Manuals and cheat sheets
    ____ Canned tutorials
    ____ Teleconferencing
    ____ Webinars
    ____ Electronic discussion lists, blogs, and wikis
    ____ Internet-based courses

V. Training group size
    ____ Large group for informational training
    ____ Small group to allow hands-on training, especially for technology training
    ____ One-on-one for highly complex training

VI. Responsibility for continuing education (e.g. fiscal, administrative, finding sources of training, etc.)
    ____ List the institution's responsibility
    ____ List staff member's responsibility

VII. Keys to success
    ____ Determine relevancy of the program
    ____ Be sure reasons for attendance are clear
    ____ Be sure program objectives are clear
    ____ Ensure that staff undergoes adequate preparation
    ____ Make sure learning is contextual
    ____ Determine if social transmission occurs during training
    ____ Make sure all learning styles are supported
    ____ Make sure good visuals and handouts for reinforcement are included

VIII. Funding provider for continuing education
    ____ Employer
      ____ Subsidy
      ____ Supplement
      ____ Incentives
      ____ Paid release time
    ____ Employee
      ____ Grants
      ____ Loans
      ____ Savings

IX. **Assessing the needs**
- ____ Employee evaluations
- ____ Surveys
- ____ Consultant review of workplace
- ____ Input from staff meetings

X. **Benefits of continuing education**
A. Direct benefit
- ____ Learning a task
- ____ Better understanding of a new system, technology, or process

B. Intangible benefits
- ____ Stimulation by new ideas
- ____ Networking with colleagues
- ____ More self confident in dealing with diverse situations and problem solving
- ____ Increased productivity and loyalty to the organization that has shown a willingness to invest in employees

SELECTED BIBLIOGRAPHY

Avery, Elizabeth Fuseler, Terry Dahlin, and Deborah A. Carver. *Staff Development: A Practical Guide.* 3rd ed. Chicago: ALA, 2001.

Brown, M. Suzanne, and Trudi Di Trolio. "The Staff Development Program at the University of Florida." *Education Libraries* 23, no. 2-3 (1999): 19–24.

Intner, Sheila S., and Janet Swan Hill, eds. *Recruiting, Educating, and Training Cataloging Librarians: Solving the Problems.* New York: Greenwood, 1989.

Intner, Sheila S., and Peggy Johnson, eds. *Recruiting, Educating, and Training Librarians for Collection Development.* Westport, Conn.: Greenwood, 1994.

Locke, Joanne. "Staff Training and Development: An Expressed Need." *Education Libraries* 23, no. 2-3 (1999): 7–8.

Seago, Kate. "Investing in People Resources: Ways and Means of Training." *Kentucky Libraries* 62, no. 2 (Spring 1998): 15–17.

Notes

Best Practices

CAROL ZSULYA
Head, Access and Distance Library Services
Cleveland State University Library

Best practices are models of ways to do things that can serve as guidelines or benchmarks for assessing your department for accomplishing the same goals as the model procedures, programs, or organizations. One key to successful use of best practices is to look for common characteristics rather than detailed procedures. For example, in looking at preprocessing, the best practices do not specify the vendor or process, but rather whether the characteristics of having books arrive shelf-ready are effective. Best practices are selected through wide consultation beyond your library, creating a consensus of professional judgment. They are a continuum along which you can judge where your library falls. Besides determining where your library fits in relation to the model, this allows you to select the parts of your program you wish to change and improve. Best practices can be used to identify the characteristics that need to change to improve outcomes. Also, best practices are relative. What works in one library may not work in the type or circumstances of another.

As a new supervisor, you will need to develop a set of best practices for your staff in technical services. Because best practices are documented strategies or tactics successfully used by a department or individual, they are processes or methods that represent the most effective way to achieve a specific objective. By identifying and sharing best practices with staff, you help your department replace poor practices, raise the performance of poor performers, and yield better productivity and efficiency. A checklist of best practices may provide a satisfying and accountable way to maximize what you and your department and staff will be doing. You will also be able to evaluate the various functions and sections of your department and make changes that fit with the mission and vision of your library.

BEGIN WITH YOUR LIBRARY

   I. **Identify your department's role and purpose within the library**
         ____ Identify specific areas within your department
            ____ Services
            ____ Functions
            ____ Staff

        ____ Technology

        ____ Policies and procedures

   ____ Identify areas of need

        ____ Services

        ____ Functions

        ____ Staff

        ____ Technology

        ____ Policies and procedures

II. Evaluate the needs

   ____ Determine the current culture of the department

   ____ Determine what changes need to be made in the culture of the department

   ____ Determine what is working and why

   ____ Determine what is not working and why

   ____ Determine if there is duplication of work by staff

   ____ Consider what other libraries' departments do

III. Establish skills and capabilities necessary for your department

   ____ Observe staff performing specific tasks

   ____ Determine if the current staff performs the appropriate tasks

   ____ Consider requiring further training to fulfill these tasks

   ____ Consider whether new staff are needed

        ____ Use cross training as an alternative to accomplish appropriate tasks by current staff

        ____ Decide if hiring new staff is necessary

IV. Establish a method to ensure changes will be made and staff will be held accountable

   ____ Set criteria for outstanding work, minimum work, and below minimum work

        ____ Attendance

        ____ Meeting deadlines

        ____ Working with others

        ____ Professional development

   ____ Set a timeline for evaluating staff, perhaps an initial six-month review, followed by annual reviews

IDENTIFY, EVALUATE, AND IMPLEMENT BEST PRACTICES FOR YOUR STAFF AND DEPARTMENT

V. Identify existing best practices

   ____ Interview your supervisor

   ____ Interview other supervisors or work groups in your department

   ____ Interview your staff

   ____ Identify the tools, processes, and systems that support these potential best practices

        ____ Decide what is working and why

        ____ Decide what is not working and why

   ____ Review published literature where available

   ____ Visit other libraries to view their procedures, functions, and organization

   ____ Survey professional colleagues through appropriate electronic discussion lists

   ____ Interview library leaders known in the field

   ____ Record your observations

VI. Codify best practices

   ____ Concentrate on a small number of high-payoff activities that can be translated into standards

_____ Develop core procedures and standards for:
  _____ Acquisitions
  _____ Cataloging
  _____ Serials
  _____ Physical processing
  _____ Bindery
  _____ Preservation
  _____ Systems
  _____ Courier services

VII. Train and coach staff
  _____ Share best practices with staff
  _____ Cross-train staff if necessary
  _____ Be open to feedback from staff; encourage them to develop and share best practices

VIII. Constantly review best practices
  _____ Periodically identify and capture improvements to existing best practices
  _____ Watch your best performers, who are likely to develop new best practices

SELECTED BIBLIOGRAPHY

Carpenter, Kathryn H. "Best Practices in Libraries—Not Just Another Edition of 'How I Done it Good': An Interview with Tom Kirk." _Library Administration & Management_ 16, no 2: (Spring 2002): 66–68.

O'Dell, Carla, and C. Jackson Grayson. "If Only We Knew What We Know: Identification and Transfer of Internal Best Practices." _California Management Review_ 40, no. 3 (Spring 1998): 154–74.

Olian, Judy D., et al. "Designing Management Training and Development for Competitive Advantage: Lessons from the Best." _Human Resource Planning_ 21, no. 1 (1998): 20–31.

U.S. General Accounting Office. "Human Capital: Effective Use of Flexibilities Can Assist Agencies in Managing Their Workforces." _GAO Reports, GAO-03-2_ (Dec. 2002): 1–62.

Zairi, Mohamed, and Yasar F. Jarrar. "Measuring Organizational Effectiveness in the NHS: Management Style and Structure Best Practices." _Total Quality Management_ 12, no. 7 (Dec. 2001): 882–89.

Notes

PERSONNEL

Coaching

MELORA RANNEY NORMAN
Outreach/Special Services Coordinator
Maine State Library

In recent decades, management styles have been evolving away from top-down systems of strict hierarchy, discipline, and cause-and-effect toward team styles and intrinsic motivation. Coaching, counseling, and mentoring—which often overlap and intertwine—are three terms that describe systems of supportive activities that are used to encourage staff self-improvement and excellence on the job.

A coach proceeds from the assumption that employees want to do well and grow on the job, both as people and as workers. Good coaching will help your employees see strengths and challenges, acknowledge and appreciate those qualities, and build upon them to improve workplace performance. As a result of coaching, employees will see not only what they need to change to better themselves, but will realize that this effort will result in better workplace satisfaction, improved opportunities for growth and career advancement, and a more significant, worthwhile role within the unit and as part of the larger organization.

Employee coaching ranges from formal, short-term programs involving consultants to ongoing efforts by managers to create positive, communicative relationships with employees. Frequently, being coached helps to make a good coach; hence, a program for coaching managers is often considered an important workplace initiative.

I. **Decide what kind of coaching is needed (or combination thereof)**
    _____ Short-term, structured
    _____ Long-term, ongoing

II. **Decide who will coach**
    _____ Manager
    _____ Peer
    _____ Consultant
    _____ Mentor
    _____ Team

III. The manager should

    ____ Act as a good role model

    ____ Create an open, supportive workplace environment

    ____ Clearly communicate expectations

    ____ Provide adequate feedback

    ____ Make coaching a part of the annual performance appraisal process

IV. When you coach

    ____ Make clear to employees the big picture context and where they fit in

    ____ Help employees understand where and why their actions or behavior are holding them back

    ____ Help employees understand where and why their actions or behavior make a negative or positive contribution to the workplace

    ____ Listen carefully to employees to be sure you are operating from the same set of assumptions

    ____ Involve employees in decisions

    ____ Initiate supportive yet honest behaviors, giving praise where appropriate

    ____ Agree upon a development plan

V. Avoid

    ____ Assuming that employees agree with your assessment of what they need to do

    ____ Imposing your own demands or views and proceeding without employees' buy-in

    ____ Making employees' mistakes into an opportunity to chastise rather than to learn and grow

    ____ Threatening negative consequences if certain results are not achieved (help employees to see the natural, not the imposed, consequences of behavior; for example, demonstrate that more efficient handling of a process will speed up processing, as opposed to threatening to write them up if they don't move faster.)

SELECTED BIBLIOGRAPHY

Avery, Elizabeth Fuseler, Terry Dahlin, and Deborah A. Carver. *Staff Development: A Practical Guide.* 3rd ed. Chicago: ALA, 2001.

Bell, Chip R. *Managers as Mentors: Building Partnerships for Learning.* San Francisco, Calif.: Berrett-Koehler, 2002.

Buzzotta, Victor R., et al. "Coaching and Counseling: How You Can Improve the Way It's Done." *Training and Development* 31, no. 11 (November 1977): 50–60.

Cook, Marshall. *Effective Coaching.* New York: McGraw-Hill, 1999.

Curzon, Suzan C. *Managing Change: A How-To-Do-It Manual for Librarians.* Rev. ed. New York: Neal-Schuman, 2005.

Dash, Julekha. "Coaching to Aid IT Careers, Retention." *Computerworld* 34, no. 12 (Mar. 20, 2000): 52.

Evans, G. Edward. *Performance Management and Appraisal: A How-To-Do-It Manual for Librarians.* New York: Neal-Schuman, 2004.

Johnson, W. Brad. *The Elements of Mentoring.* New York: Palgrave Macmillan, 2004.

Leeds, Dorothy. "Training One-on-One." *Training and Development* 50, no. 9 (Sept. 1996): 42–44.

Logan, David Colman. *The Coaching Revolution: How Visionary Managers Are Using Coaching to Empower People and Unlock Their Full Potential.* Holbrook, Mass.: Adams Media, 2001.

Metz, Ruth F. *Coaching in the Library: A Management Strategy for Achieving Excellence.* Chicago: ALA, 2001.

Phillips, Kenneth R. "The Achilles Heel of Coaching." *Training and Development* 52, no. 3 (Mar. 1998): 41–44.

Stone, Florence M. *Coaching, Counseling & Mentoring: How To Choose & Use the Right Technique To Boost Employee Performance.* New York: AMACOM, 1999.

Stowell, Steven J. "Coaching: A Commitment to Leadership." *Training and Development* 42, no. 6 (Jun. 1988): 34–38.

Sujansky, Joanne. "The Critical Care and Feeding of Generation Y." *Workforce* 81, no. 5 (May 2002): 15.

Delegation

ALTHEA ASCHMAN
Head of Cataloging
Virginia Tech University

Delegation is entrusting another person with sufficient power and authority to get the work done or act on the manager's behalf. To delegate effectively, you must assign a task or responsibility and give your employees sufficient authority to complete the assignment. The employees then become accountable for completion of the assignment, and you have the responsibility to enforce that accountability. Delegation takes practice—it is a skill learned by doing. You may overcome barriers to delegation and excuses for failure to delegate by self-examination and just trying it again and again.

Delegation is at the heart of management—it is getting work done and meeting goals through others. It is about developing trust and empowering employees. Effective delegation increases productivity as well as production capacity. J. C. Penney once said that the wisest decision he ever made was to "let go," after realizing he could no longer do everything by himself. That decision allowed for the growth of a company with hundreds of stores and thousands of people. Effective delegation will allow you more discretionary time to focus on high priority matters to which only you should attend. In other words, delegation is one of the most high leverage activities there is.

I. Preparation

____ Develop confidence in yourself and security about your position in the organization (this will take time, but is necessary for sustained effectiveness)

____ Be willing to take calculated risks

____ Learn from mistakes

____ Trust employees to do their jobs

    ____ Know the skill and experience levels and limitations of employees

    ____ Allow employees to use their own ideas or methods to complete assignments

____ Be able to explain an assignment and the desired results

____ Develop a mechanism for progress reports and feedback

____ Be patient; results take time

____ Provide support and resources to employees

II. Considerations for decisions to delegate

____ Individual employee abilities

____ Routine or recurring types of tasks

____ Information or data collection

____ Amount of details requiring attention and employee suitability for detailed work

____ Employee potential to assume additional or more complex responsibilities

____ Cost effectiveness

____ Employee interest

____ Potential for facilitating employee development with the assignment

____ Empowerment of a work group

____ Delegation of the tasks that help increase productivity

____ Delegation of the tasks that help you deal with time pressures

____ Your willingness to take the time and effort to be skillful in turning over a job to an employee

III. Do not delegate

____ Explanation and delegation of assignments to subordinates

____ Performance evaluations

____ Disciplinary actions

____ Addressing performance and morale problems

____ Confidential or sensitive tasks

____ Tasks your supervisor requests specifically that you complete

____ Tasks that put employees in confusing or complex situations

IV. Selection of assignments and people

____ Outline skill requirements

____ Determine who has the requisite skills

____ Select employees who show interest

____ Keep employee workload manageable and clarify priorities

____ Match tasks to people

____ Avoid favoritism or excessive dependence on any one employee

____ Determine the best choice for completion of an assignment or project

    ____ Team

    ____ Group

    ____ Individual

V. Assignment of responsibilities

____ Clearly explain the goals and objectives of the assignment

    ____ The goal is the overall results desired

    ____ Objectives are intermediate steps to reach a goal

    ____ If you cannot articulate these, more preparation is needed before delegation

____ Be sure employees have a clear understanding of the assignment

    ____ Confirm the assignment in writing

    ____ Have written policies and procedures for routine or recurring tasks

    ____ Have employees explain their understanding of the assignment and desired outcome

    ____ Follow up periodically and monitor employees' progress

____ Assign priority and importance levels. Explain these to employees

____ Articulate the timetable and deadlines

____ Point out potential complications, obstacles, and pitfalls

____ Be results-oriented, and remember the outcome is what matters, not the method of getting there

_____ Observe the exception when something must follow a specific protocol
_____ Establish clear performance expectations
    _____ Realistic and obtainable
    _____ Agreed on standards and guidelines
    _____ Accountability
        _____ Performance contract
        _____ Progress reports
        _____ Monitoring progress
        _____ Quality of completed assignment
        _____ Giving employees the freedom to act, but making them accountable for the results
    _____ Articulate consequences by specifying what will happen, both good and bad, as a result of performance or assignment evaluation and the natural consequences tied into the overall mission of the organization
_____ Assign the level of authority
    _____ Choose one
        _____ Act after approval
        _____ Inform and act
        _____ Act and report
        _____ Act with partial authority
        _____ Act with complete authority
    _____ Avoid after-the-fact approval or disapproval
_____ Provide support
    _____ Resources
        _____ Identify people who can assist with the task
        _____ Identify available information resources
        _____ Supply needed equipment and supplies
        _____ Allow sufficient time for assignment completion
    _____ Key individuals with whom employees will need to work are contacted and informed of their roles
    _____ Managerial support
        _____ Be sincere when offering assistance
        _____ Discuss in advance what role you will take
        _____ Tell employees what concerns they can bring to you
        _____ Encourage employees to develop alternatives for action rather than simply bringing problems to you and requesting a solution
        _____ Teach employees things they can do to become less dependent on you
_____ Practice stewardship delegation
    _____ Allow employees to take ownership of the project or assignment
    _____ Trust the employee to get the job done
    _____ Stay results-oriented and keep responsibility for results with employee
    _____ Avoid "go for" or "get me this, get me that" delegation
    _____ Encourage innovation
    _____ Clarify roles when more than one person is on an assignment, or enable a mechanism for them to do so themselves to avoid work overlap
    _____ Make interesting assignments when possible
    _____ Do not delegate only boring or routine tasks, which compromises credibility and lowers morale
_____ Let employees know you value their time; show it in both words and actions

VI. **Barriers to effective delegation and excuses to avoid**

_____ "It is easier to do it myself, and I know it'll be done right if I do it"

_____ "I don't have confidence in _____"

_____ "I'm afraid what my boss will think"

_____ Fear of being disliked by subordinates

_____ Perfectionism and intolerance for mistakes

_____ Need to feel in control or fear of losing control

_____ Need to feel important or be perceived as a super worker

_____ Fear of becoming unneeded or being replaced

_____ Insecurity

_____ Opinion that delegation takes too much time or effort

_____ Preference for doing, rather than planning

_____ Failure to delegate authority commensurate with responsibilities

_____ Difficulty in balancing the workload

_____ Failure to establish effective controls and follow up

_____ Urgency or crisis management

VII. **Other issues that may need to be addressed**

_____ Training for personnel lacking experience or needed skills

_____ Work overload

_____ Disorganization

_____ Immersion in trivia

_____ Excessive dependence on the manager

_____ Lack of commitment to organizational goals

_____ Confusion about responsibilities and authority

_____ Understaffing

SELECTED BIBLIOGRAPHY

Beck, Arthur C., and Ellis D. Hillmar. *Positive Management Practices.* Jossey-Bass Management Series. San Francisco, Calif.: Jossey-Bass, 1986. Chapters 6,8,9, and 10 relate to delegation.

Blanchard, Ken, John P. Carlos, and Alan Randolph. *Empowerment Takes More than a Minute.* 2nd ed. San Francisco, Calif.: Barrett-Koehler, 2001.

Burns, Robert B. *Making Delegation Happen: A Simple and Effective Guide to Implementing Successful Delegation.* Crow's Nest, New South Wales, Australia: Allen and Unwin, 2001.

Covey, Stephen R. "Delegation, Increasing P and PC," in *The 7 Habits of Highly Effective People,* 171–79. New York: Simon and Schuster, 1990.

———. "Agreements," in *The 7 Habits of Highly Effective People,* 223–24.

Longenecker, Clinton O., and Jack L. Simonetti. *Getting Results: Five Absolutes for High Performance.* Univ. of Michigan Business School Management Series. San Francisco, Calif.: Jossey-Bass, 2001.

Nelson, Bob. *Please Don't Just Do What I Tell You, Do What Needs To Be Done! Every Employee's Guide to Making Work More Rewarding.* New York: Hyperion, 2001.

Nelson, Robert B., and Peter Fiore. *Delegation: Goal Attainment through Others.* New York: Training by Design, 1984.

Nelson, Robert B. *Delegation: The Power of Letting Go.* Glenview, Ill.: Scott, Foresman, 1988.

Discipline

ANDREA KAPPLER
Cataloging Manager
Evansville Vanderburgh Public Library

Disciplining employees is an unpleasant but necessary task every manager faces from time to time. In a perfect world, your employees would always do their jobs all the time without any problems or follow-up. In the real world, employees sometimes lose interest in their job duties or face other issues that cause their behavior to change or their standards of work to decline.

Before disciplining an employee, make sure that there is a clearly defined, written job description for the position and that the employee understands it and has a copy of it. Also make sure everyone has a copy of the library's written employee guidelines to avoid questions about expected and acceptable behavior. Without employee guidelines or a written job description, enforcing rule violations or performance standards is difficult. Your relationship with employees should be collaborative, not antagonistic.

Maintain written documentation to record the positive and negative performance and behavior of all employees. Doing this may be time-consuming, but it allows more objective assessments about staff. If legal counsel is ever needed, documentation becomes invaluable.

I. **General employee guidelines**
   _____ Provide new employees with a copy of library personnel guidelines
   _____ Meet with new employees to answer questions about personnel guidelines
   _____ If the library changes personnel guidelines, make sure your staff know what has changed and receive or have access to written copies of changed policies

II. **Job responsibilities, goals, and performance reviews**
   _____ Provide a written job description
   _____ Meet with the employees regularly and set challenging but achievable goals for their jobs
   _____ Conduct regular performance reviews so that positive behavior and performance are recorded

III. **Rule violations or performance problems**
   _____ Witness a rule violation first-hand, if possible

_____ Document the incident immediately after it occurs

    _____ Record the rule violation or performance problem

        _____ Keep a written log in a password-protected file in a computer program (e.g., Word, Excel)

        _____ Keep a written log in a file in a locked drawer

    _____ Record the date, time, and location of the problem

    _____ Conduct a brief oral counseling session in private as soon as possible to correct the behavior or performance problem

        _____ Stick with the facts relating to the situation

        _____ Listen to the employee

        _____ Be direct and specific with feedback, and coach the employee toward improvement

        _____ Document the discussion to eliminate problems of recall and distortion of information

_____ If behavior or performance does not improve after an oral counseling session, develop a written memorandum

    _____ Outline the rule violation or performance problem. Use quantifiable terms whenever possible

    _____ Include only facts and clearly observable behavior

    _____ Provide specific, measurable steps to correct the problem and a reasonable timeframe for those steps to be completed

    _____ Provide reasonable consequences if the employee does not improve performance within the stated timeframe

    _____ Meet with the employee privately, and discuss the memo individually

        _____ Set a friendly, inquiring tone, and establish from the outset that you expect a give-and-take discussion

        _____ Describe in objective terms how the employee's behavior or performance fails to meet acceptable standards

        _____ Listen to the employee

        _____ Be positive about the employee's ability to improve

    _____ Ask the employee to sign the memo. Keep a copy for your files, send a copy to the personnel department, and give the employee a copy

_____ If you have included a timeline in which to improve, meet at the end of that time to give feedback on progress

    _____ Discuss whether the behavior or performance has improved

    _____ If behavior or performance has not improved, determine if termination may be necessary

IV. Termination of an employee

_____ Make sure all positive and negative performances and behaviors are documented

_____ Inform your supervisor before you act

_____ Prepare a written memo

    _____ Outline the rule violation or performance problem. Use quantifiable terms whenever possible

    _____ Include only facts and clearly observable behavior

_____ Plan the interview so that it will not fall on a Friday, after the employee returns from vacation, or on the person's birthday or anniversary

_____ Meet with the employee privately. Limit the interview to no more than ten minutes

_____ Deliver the news clearly and unemotionally

_____ Collect the employee's identification card, name badge, office keys, confidential files, and any company property the person may have used off the premises

_____ Cancel passwords to computer programs and e-mail accounts

_____ After the termination, refuse to discuss any aspects of the termination or the employee's performance or conduct with third parties such as other employees or prospective employers

SELECTED BIBLIOGRAPHY

Berryman-Fink, Cynthia. _The Manager's Desk Reference._ 2nd ed. New York: AMACOM, 1996.

Chapman, Elwood N. _The Fifty-Minute Supervisor._ 2nd ed. Los Altos, Calif.: Crisp Pubs., 1988.

Cottringer, William. "The ABCs of Employee Discipline." _Supervision_ 64, no. 4 (Apr. 2003): 5-7.

Crittendon, Robert. _The New Manager's Starter Kit: Essential Tools for Doing the Job Right._ New York: AMACOM, 2002.

DelPo, Amy, and Lisa Guerin. _Dealing with Problem Employees: A Legal Guide._ 3rd ed. Berkeley, Calif.: Nolo Pr., 2005.

Falcone, Paul. _101 Sample Write-ups for Documenting Employee Performance Problems: A Guide to Progressive Discipline & Termination._ New York: AMACOM, 1999.

———. _The Hiring and Firing Question and Answer Book._ New York: AMACOM, 2002.

Freemantle, David. _The New A–Z of Managing People._ Holbrook, Mass.: Adams Media, 1999.

Hendricks, William, ed. _Coaching, Mentoring, and Managing._ Franklin Lakes, N.J.: Career Pr., 1996.

Sachs, Randi Toler. _Productive Performance Appraisals._ New York: AMACOM, 1992.

Smigel, Lloyd Merritt. _Basic Training for New Managers._ Los Angeles: Lowell House, 2000.

Stettner, Morey. _Skills for New Managers._ New York: McGraw-Hill, 2000.

Straub, Joseph T. _The Rookie Manager: A Guide to Surviving Your First Year in Management._ New York: AMACOM, 2000.

Sweet, Donald H. _A Manager's Guide to Conducting Terminations: Minimizing Emotional Stress and Legal Risks._ Lexington, Mass.: Lexington Bks., 1989.

Notes

Goal Setting

EMILY BERGMAN
Head of Collections and Access Services
Occidental College

A goal is a specific and measurable accomplishment to be achieved within a specified time and under particular constraints. It is an end toward which your employees will willingly expend some effort. What kind of and how much effort is always related to the goal itself, by being able to identify the cost and benefit relationship. Planning an analysis of the elements of the goal is the way to decide if it is worth achieving.

Initiate the goal setting process by starting with where the employee is. The clearer the goals, the stronger the motivation will be to accomplish these goals; nebulous thoughts must be translated into the concrete. Accomplishment takes less time when energy is focused on specific action than it does when acting without planning or motivation.

Commit to completing the actions by specific dates and then to reviewing your employees' progress every few weeks until everything is accomplished. This is extremely important; otherwise, they will feel further action is no longer necessary and may lose sight of the goals that have been set.

I. **Elements of a goal**
    _____ Goals can be anything so long as they contribute to the mission
    _____ Goals identify direction
    _____ Goals are developed from
        _____ Needs
        _____ Roles
        _____ Responsibilities
    _____ Goals should be stated in positive rather than negative terms
    _____ Goals should be
        _____ Realistic
        _____ Practical
        _____ Achievable
    _____ Goals have quantifiable outcomes so you can measure progress, including when and
          how much progress is expected

_____ Define objectives for reaching the goal, including how to achieve the goal

_____ Commit sufficient resources for reaching the goal, including people, funding, equipment, commitment, etc.

_____ Design contingency plans to deal with potential obstacles that have been identified

_____ Difficult goals have more productive results than easy goals

     _____ Performance increases as goals become more difficult

     _____ Persistence increases as goals become more difficult

_____ Set goals to guide action, not as a device for punishment

II. Creating goals

_____ Have employees take the lead in setting their goals. They will be more successful if they feel the goals are their own

_____ Make goals clear and concrete, and be sure they are written down

     _____ Specific goals direct action more reliably than vague or general goals

     _____ Goal specificity results in clear expectations

_____ Start with short-range goals that are more within control and easily attainable

_____ Set realistic deadlines

_____ Break a large goal into manageable units

III. Setting priorities

_____ Set priorities regularly

_____ Establish priorities on long-term as well as short-term bases

_____ Use criteria to establish priorities

     _____ Evaluate the facts

     _____ Incorporate flexible criteria

     _____ Be accurate

     _____ Remember the 80/20 rule: Of all the things that could be done to reach goals, about 20 percent of the current effort probably yields 80 percent of the results

     _____ Rank concerns by importance and urgency

_____ Regularly work on the high-priority issues

_____ Communicate priorities to others who are affected by the actions

IV. Working on goals

_____ Look for the potential problems that may be roadblocks to reaching goals

_____ Take action to remove or minimize those potential problems

_____ Know what resources are needed to reach the goals

_____ Work toward goals that are compatible with one another

_____ Be comfortable asking for help to reach goals

_____ Accept the responsibility for working toward goals

_____ Minimize interruptions that get in the way of reaching goals

_____ Be flexible to changes that affect the progress toward goals

_____ Be persistent about working toward goals

_____ Pursue those activities that are related to reaching goals

V. Common goal achievement obstacles

A. Procrastination

_____ The danger is in the inactivity, delaying work, and/or taking no actions to bring goal achievement closer

_____ The longer one procrastinates, the more pressure is created on the timeline for goal achievement as expressed in the deadline of the goal statement

_____ Pressure often encourages you to take shortcuts or to settle for less than complete goal satisfaction

_____ Procrastination can be avoided

    _____ Have sufficient motivation to achieve the goal

    _____ Establish clear priorities for identified tasks

    _____ Break needed tasks into smaller components

    _____ Set mini-deadlines for each task

    _____ Provide rewards when tasks are completed

B. Unproductive activities

    _____ Do not just do things; do the right things

    _____ Establish clear, focused goal statements

    _____ Perform only those tasks that meet objectives and result in moving closer to goal achievement; just being busy does not necessarily meet the goal

    _____ Review the results, priorities, and plans that contribute to reaching established goals

C. Goal difficulty

    _____ Requires more hours

    _____ Involves greater risk

    _____ Has greater possibility of failure

D. Other obstacles

    _____ Goal overload

    _____ Goal conflicts

    _____ Goal ambiguity

    _____ Excessive risk taking that can be controlled by a risk analysis

    _____ Fear of taking risks

    _____ Failure, which may undermine self-confidence but can be remedied by treating failure as a problem to be solved rather than a signal to punish

    _____ Goals treated as ceilings rather than minimums

    _____ Short-range thinking

    _____ Dishonesty and cheating

    _____ Lack of training in the areas for which the goals are set

VI. **Accomplishing goals**

A. Implement the plan

    _____ Plan carefully and comprehensively

    _____ Execute the plan

B. Monitor progress

    _____ Review progress periodically

        _____ Use people who can provide objective viewpoints about accomplishments, celebrate successes, and help with any problems that may be experienced

        _____ Consider setting up the review process on a contract basis

        _____ Include in performance appraisals

    _____ Measure planned versus actual results

    _____ Determine which elements work and which do not work

C. Revise objectives

    _____ Change tactics, if conditions change

    _____ Apply what works

D. Goals must be supported

    _____ By supervisors

    _____ By employee

    _____ By departmental coworkers

E. Success is facilitated by positive incentives; negative incentives, such as losing one's job, has a negative effect on goal acceptance. Positive incentives include:

____ Anticipation or challenge of the job

____ Pride in accomplishment

____ Recognition

____ Feedback

____ Pleasing the boss

____ Money

SELECTED BIBLIOGRAPHY

"Encourage Employees to Commit to Goals." *Leadership for the Front Lines* 425 (Nov. 1, 2001): 8.

Ford, George A. *Creating Your Future: A Guide to Personal Goal Setting.* San Diego, Calif.: University Associates, 1988.

Fouillard, Larrie. *Goals and Goal Setting.* Menlo Park, Calif.: Crisp,1998.

Locke, Edwin A., and Gary P. Latham. *Goal Setting: A Motivational Technique That Works!* Englewood Cliffs, N.J.: Prentice-Hall, 1984.

Smith, Douglas K. *Make Success Measurable!: A Mindbook-Workbook for Setting Goals and Taking Action.* New York: Wiley, 1999.

"Tips for Setting Training Goals." *Leadership for the Front Lines* 425 (May 1, 2002): 7.

Wadsworth, Walter J. *The Agile Manager's Guide to Goal-setting and Achievement.* Bristol, Vt.: Velocity Business Pub., 1997.

Wilson, Susan B. *Goal Setting.* New York: American Management Association, 1994.

Zimmer, Ron. "A Goal is A Dream with A Deadline." *Information Executive* 7, no. 3 (May/Jun. 2003): 1.

Job Descriptions

NANCY LEE MYERS
Acquisitions Librarian and Professor
University of South Dakota

A job description is more than an abstract of a job breakdown containing the essential activities, classification, and requirements. It is used in classifying and evaluating jobs and in the recruitment, selection, placement, and evaluation of employees. It usually begins with a job analysis using interviews with a current employee, if there is one, and critical examination of the essential responsibilities and functions of the job, the qualifications needed, the reporting hierarchy, and other important aspects of the job. While usually thought of as an internal document, the job description is actually affected by many outside influences, such as unions and the Americans with Disabilities Act (ADA). Because a job description is an important document with legal ramifications for the individual and the institution, it must be written carefully and updated as the job changes.

I. **Analyze the job**
    ____ Interview with incumbent
        ____ Determine essential functions of the position
            ____ Function is highly specialized, and the person in the position must have the qualifications to perform it (e.g., a cataloger of Russian books must have the ability to translate Russian.)
            ____ The number of employees available to perform the function is limited (e.g., materials need repair, and there is one preservation assistant, so being able to work on books and paper are essential functions)
            ____ The position exists to perform the function (e.g., the acquisitions librarian is hired to order library resources, so the ability to order library resources is an essential function)
            ____ Removal of the function would fundamentally change the position
            ____ The function is performed frequently or takes up substantial amounts of time
            ____ Failure to perform the function would have serious consequences
        ____ Determine functions the incumbent may have been performing due to unique qualifications

_____ Gather information about the position
     _____ Supervisor's title
     _____ Basic purpose of the job
     _____ Most important duties of the position
     _____ Percentage of time spent on each duty
     _____ Additional responsibilities performed in the position
     _____ Equipment and materials used in the position
     _____ Decision-making requirements of the position
     _____ Record-keeping or reports required of the position
     _____ Supervision of other employees
          _____ List number of employees
          _____ Give employees' job titles
     _____ Educational background, experience, or skills required

II. Outside influences to consider

_____ The ADA prohibits discrimination in employment against qualified people who have disabilities, and it requires identification of the essential functions of each job and reasonable accommodation to the disabilities of qualified candidates. The required qualifications listed on the job description must support the essential functions of the job and serve as the criteria for selection of candidates. An accommodation is considered reasonable, unless it imposes an undue hardship upon the library (undue hardship is defined as significant difficulty, costly, or disruptive)

_____ Affirmative Action/Equal Employment Opportunity Guidelines. The United States Equal Employment Opportunity Commission mandates first that the candidate possesses the required qualifications (e.g., education, experience, or skills), and second, that the candidate be able to perform the essential functions of the job with or without reasonable accommodation. Results, rather than the method used to achieve them, is the litmus test

_____ All applicable local and state laws that affect employment at your library. Your human resources department should be able to provide information about these

_____ Collective bargaining agreements and employee unions. Your human resources department should have a copy of the current contract, and you should take time to review it thoroughly

III. The job description

A. Contents

_____ Job title
_____ Primary purpose of the job
_____ Principal duties, percentage of time required, and accountabilities
_____ Position in the hierarchy of library and working relationships (i.e., subordinate roles, supervisory roles, others)
_____ Equipment used to perform the job
_____ Minimal qualifications necessary to perform essential functions
_____ Salary range (optional)

B. Style

_____ Clear sentences using present tense verbs (e.g., "Records departmental statistics accurately")
_____ Explanatory phrases where necessary (e.g., "Records departmental statistics accurately on a monthly basis")
_____ Unambiguous words (e.g., monthly), rather than words subject to differing interpretations, (e.g., frequently)

_____ Unbiased terminology (e.g., he/she)

IV. **Uses of the job description**
_____ Basis for identifying reasonable accommodations for disabled persons
_____ Advertising and recruitment aid
_____ Tool for determining whether candidates are qualified
_____ Basis for determining compensation
_____ Training guide
_____ Basis for performance reviews
_____ Source of structure within the library
_____ Protection for the library from legal claims

SELECTED BIBLIOGRAPHY

Barlow, Wayne E., and Edward Z. Hane. "A Practical Guide to the Americans with Disabilities Act." _Personnel Journal_ 7, no. 6 (1992): 53–60.

Baron, James N., and David M. Kreps. _Strategic Human Resources: Frameworks for General Managers._ New York: Wiley, 1999.

Duston, Robert L., Karen S. Russell, and Lynn E. Kerr. _A Guide to Writing Job Descriptions under the Americans with Disabilities Act._ Washington, D.C.: College and University Personnel Association, 1992.

Moravec, Milan, and Robert Tucker. "Job Descriptions for the 21st Century." _Personnel Journal_ 7, no. 6 (1992): 37–44.

Ray, Tom H., and Pat Hawthorne, compilers. _Librarian Job Descriptions in ARL Libraries: A SPEC Kit._ SPEC Kit 194. Washington, D.C.: Association of Research Libraries, 1993.

Sims, Ronald R. _Organizational Success through Effective Human Resources Management._ Westport, Conn.: Quorum Bks., 2002.

Zenelis, John G., and Jean M. Dorrian, compilers. _Non-Librarian Professionals: A SPEC Kit._ SPEC Kit 212. Washington, D.C.: Association of Research Libraries, 1995.

Notes

Motivating Staff

SHARON CASTLEBERRY
Systems Librarian
DeSoto Public Library

Your job as a manager in the workplace is to get things done through your employees. In most institutions, staff salaries and benefits account for the largest portion of the annual operating budget. The success of the organization may be directly traced to the success of its employees; therefore, it is critical that you be able to motivate staff to bring about the best performance. However, this is easier said than done! You must understand what type of rewards and recognition are most valued by your staff and be able to furnish these reinforcements. An organization staffed with highly motivated individuals is almost sure to be a successful one, both for its customers and employees.

Motivation practice and theory are difficult subjects, touching on several disciplines. Many options are available to motivate staff; presented here are six broad, often-recognized strategies.

I. **Positive reinforcements**
   - _____ Personally thank employees for doing a good job
   - _____ Inspire and encourage staff
   - _____ Recognize achievements
   - _____ Celebrate successes of the department and the individual
   - _____ Make work fun
   - _____ Promote camaraderie
   - _____ Take time for team and morale building meetings and activities
   - _____ Use incentives

II. **Satisfying employee needs**
   - _____ Take time to meet with and listen to each employee
   - _____ Encourage ideas and discussion
   - _____ Create an open and trusting work environment
   - _____ Be sincere
   - _____ Be friendly
   - _____ Recognize what is important to your team

_____ Offer a challenge
_____ Provide equipment and training that will enable greater productivity

III. Setting work-related goals

_____ Provide information about how each employee fits into the overall worksite
_____ Involve employees in decisions, especially those that affect them
_____ Encourage staff to have a sense of ownership in their work
_____ Invest people in the cause
_____ Provide an environment where employees can develop a purpose

IV. Positive job structure

_____ Create a partnership with each employee
_____ Give staff a chance to grow and learn new skills
_____ Provide a flexible work structure to allow variety in employees' job responsibilities
_____ Encourage new initiatives
_____ When possible, restructure job responsibilities according to employees' interests and skills

V. Base rewards on job performance

_____ Use performance as the basis for recognizing, rewarding, and promoting
_____ Provide a system of awards to recognize achievement (e.g., certificates, pins, etc.)
_____ Deal with low and marginal performers so they improve or leave

SELECTED BIBLIOGRAPHY

Blanchard, Ken, and Sheldon Bowles. *Gung Ho! Turn on the People in Any Organization.* New York: William Morrow and Co., 1997.

Daniels, Aubrey C. *Bringing Out the Best in People: How to Apply the Astonishing Power of Positive Reinforcement.* New York: McGraw-Hill, 2000.

Glanz, Barbara A. *Handle with Care: Motivating and Retaining Your Employees.* New York: McGraw-Hill, 2002.

Grensing-Pophal, Lin. *Motivating Today's Employees.* Billingham, Wash.: Self-Counsel Pr., 2002.

Kantor, Jan. *Inspiring People in the Workplace.* Ft. Myers Beach, Fla.: Island Pr. Pubs., 1992.

Lundin, Stephen, Harry Paul, and John Christensen. *Fish! A Remarkable Way to Boost Morale and Improve Results.* New York: Hyperion, 2000.

Nelson, Bob, and Peter Economy. *Managing for Dummies.* 2nd ed. New York: Wiley, 2003.

Ramundo, Michael, and Susan Shelly. *The Complete Idiot's Guide to Motivating People.* New York: Alpha Bks., 2000.

Weinstein, Matt. *Managing to Have Fun.* New York: Simon and Schuster, 1997.

Evaluation

MARLENE SLOUGH
Head of Acquisitions
Eastern Illinois University

Few aspects of management are as controversial as evaluation. It is a process that, in general, both the supervisor and the employee would prefer to avoid. However, decisions based on judgments must be made, and the evaluation process ensures that those decisions will be lawful, fair, defensible, and accurate. You need to familiarize yourself with the system currently in practice and educate yourself regarding the ramifications of evaluation to employees. When the process is formalized and the employee shares in the process, all parties—the employee, the supervisor, and the library—will benefit.

An ideal evaluation system probably does not exist. A good performance evaluation is *valid* if it measures performance-related behaviors and productivity and *reliable* if it provides a consistent measure of work performance. Sample evaluation forms are readily available in the literature and on the Internet. Most organizations are happy to provide copies of their evaluation forms upon request.

I. **Value of evaluation**
    - _____ To maintain services consistent with the values of the library
    - _____ To improve services consistent with the values of the library
    - _____ To provide accountability of resources
    - _____ To provide a method for planning future goals and objectives
    - _____ To provide employees with a clear understanding of job duties
    - _____ To recognize outstanding performance by employees
    - _____ To fairly compensate performance
    - _____ To fairly evaluate competence
    - _____ To provide opportunities for performance improvement
    - _____ To provide effective feedback regarding performance to the employee
    - _____ To motivate employees to do their best
    - _____ To identify employee training and development needs

II. **Uses of evaluation**
    - _____ Increased communication between supervisor and employee
    - _____ Employee motivation

_____ Coaching
_____ Compensation
_____ Promotion
_____ Merit pay distribution
_____ Reassignment
_____ Demotion
_____ Dismissal
_____ Layoff
_____ Tenure
_____ Retention

III. **Types of evaluation**
   A. Informal evaluation examples
      _____ Supervisor observations of employee productivity based on established standards
      _____ Supervisor perceptions of employee performance based on a log of positive and negative job behaviors
      _____ Peer observations of employee performance
   B. Formal evaluation examples
      _____ Top-down
      _____ Peer-to-peer
      _____ 360 degree
      _____ Self-assessment
      _____ Team
      _____ Comparative (employees are evaluated in relation to one another)
      _____ Absolute (employees are evaluated without comparison to other employees)
      _____ Outcome-based (employees are evaluated on the basis of established performance outcomes)

IV. **Evaluation interview**
   A. Before the interview
      1. As the supervisor, you should:
         _____ Study the position description
         _____ Evaluate your performance as a supervisor
         _____ Complete the written evaluation form carefully, based on continuous observation documented throughout the evaluation period
         _____ Schedule the interview, allowing the employee sufficient time to prepare
      2. As the supervisor, be sure you and the employee understand:
         _____ The nature of the evaluation instrument (tasks under review and the standards used)
         _____ To whom the form is routed
         _____ Where the form is filed
         _____ Who has access to the evaluation results
         _____ How long the evaluation form is retained
         _____ Any appeal process
         _____ The effect of the evaluation on other personnel actions
         _____ Any organization regulations or union contracts
         _____ What is legal, required, and permissible in employee performance evaluation
   B. During the interview, as the supervisor you should:
      _____ Conduct the interview in a comfortable and private environment
      _____ Allow sufficient time for the interview
      _____ Review the completed form with the employee

_____ Discuss areas for improvement
_____ Provide opportunities for employee responses
_____ Listen
_____ Discuss employee concerns
_____ Summarize the employee's strengths and weaknesses
_____ End on a positive note
_____ Secure the necessary signatures
_____ Follow up the evaluation with periodic informal reviews, but be careful not to make promises that would be hard to keep

V. **Common attributes of successful evaluations**
_____ The evaluation instrument reflects the values of your organization
_____ Both supervisor and employee understand the purpose of the evaluation
_____ Training and orientation is provided for supervisors regarding the organization's evaluation process
_____ Training and orientation is provided for employees regarding the organization's evaluation process
_____ Both supervisor and employee understand how the evaluation is used in the organization
_____ The evaluation process is perceived as fair by the supervisor and the employee
_____ The evaluation period is clearly defined
_____ Job duties and performance expectations are clearly defined
_____ The employee and supervisor have prior agreement of job duties
_____ The employee appraisal is based on continuous or ongoing assessment throughout the evaluation period
_____ The employee appraisal is based on patterns of behavior, not isolated incidents, documented throughout the evaluation period
_____ Confidentiality is maintained by the supervisor

VI. **Things to keep in mind (and avoid) as a new supervisor completing evaluations**
_____ Personal bias (i.e., unfairly judging members of different races, religion, gender, national origin, or sexual orientation)
_____ Halo effect (i.e., letting your appraisal of one factor affect your appraisal of other factors)
_____ Central tendency (i.e., judging most workers as average, thus making no distinction between good and poor performers)
_____ Harshness (i.e., judging everyone at the low end of the scale)
_____ Leniency (i.e., judging everyone at the high end of the scale)
_____ Similarity (i.e., judging people who are like you higher than people who are different from you)
_____ Turning of events (i.e., allowing what happened recently to affect your judgment of the person's performance throughout the entire evaluation period)
_____ Seniority (i.e., unfairly judging workers based on how long they have been on the job)
_____ Acquaintanceship (i.e., letting how well you know workers affect your appraisal)

SELECTED BIBLIOGRAPHY

Baldwin, David A., Frances C. Wilkinson, and Daniel C. Barkley. *Effective Management of Student Employment: Organizing for Student Employment in Academic Libraries*. Englewood, Colo.: Libraries Unlimited, 2000.

Belcastro, Patricia. *Evaluating Library Staff: A Performance Appraisal System*. Chicago: ALA, 1998.

Giesecke, Joan, ed. *Practical Help for New Supervisors*. 3rd ed. Chicago: ALA, 1997.

Goodson, Carol F. The *Complete Guide to Performance Standards for Library Personnel.* New York: Neal-Schuman,1997.

Kratz, Charles E., and Valerie A. Platz. *The Personnel Manual: An Outline for Libraries.* 2nd ed. Chicago: ALA, 1993.

Lubans, John, Jr. "'I've Closed My Eyes to the Cold Hard Truth I'm Seeing': Making Performance Appraisal Work." *Library Administration & Management* 13, no. 2 (Spring 1999): 87–89.

Maloney, Donna L. "Meeting Performance Appraisal Head-on at Chicago Public Library." *Public Libraries* 40, no. 3 (May/Jun. 2001): 178–80.

Martin, Lowell Arthur. *Library Personnel Administration.* Metuchen, N.J.: Scarecrow Pr., 1994.

Osif, Bonnie A. "Evaluation and Assessment, Part 1: Evaluation of Individuals." *Library Administration & Management* 19, no. 1 (Winter 2002): 44–48.

Russell, Carrie. "Using Performance Measurement to Evaluate Teams and Organizational Effectiveness." *Library Administration & Management* 12, no. 3 (Summer 1998): 159–65.

Assessing Strengths and Weaknesses in Staff

STEPHEN COCHRAN

Librarian

Washington State Department of Transportation

First-time managers quickly learn that employees come into the job with a set of skills and innate abilities particular to each individual. Moreover, while these skills may be perceived as strengths in certain circumstances, they will almost certainly be viewed as a weakness in others. To use the human resources available to you effectively, consider your employees' skills and talents.

A person with innate verbal skills, for example, may be viewed as *skillfully articulate* if asked to provide an inservice on the use of new cataloging software, but may be branded a *tiresome chatterbox* if unable to refrain from talking ad nauseam about each modification made to each bibliographic record. Additionally, staff that has been in place for a while will have developed skills in the routine performance of their jobs. Use of specialized software is an example of such a skill. Strengths in this area can also become weaknesses if, as often happens, changes in the specialized software are met with resistance, criticized as not as good as the old way of doing things, or—at worst—ignored.

Part of your task is to assess the existing skills of reporting staff and then orchestrate, to the best of your ability, the time and activity of staff so the skills brought to the job will be assets, not liabilities, to the department and the organization as a whole. Assessing the strengths and weaknesses of reporting staff can make the difference between a great department and a mediocre department. "Teaming people up who have complimentary or opposite strengths and weaknesses can . . . prove a beneficial way to develop a [department's] skills."[1] Pairing a cataloger who is strong on bibliographic description with one who does not handle that area well but is very competent to assign access points is an example of such a combination.

Many areas in the workplace can reveal the strengths and weaknesses of your reporting staff. If one employee takes significantly longer than others to complete the procedures associated with a particular task, the employee may need to have some skill-building work done.[2]

1. Ginger Trumfio and William Keenan, Jr., "Managing Strengths for Sales Success," Sales & Marketing Management 146, no. 10 (Oct. 1994): 43.
2. Diane Mayo and Jeanne Goodrich, *Staffing for Results: A Guide to Working Smarter* (Chicago: ALA, 2002).

Presented are lists of skills to be considered within each of these areas. Checking the item off the list indicates an employee strength; an item that cannot be given a checkmark indicates an area in which improvement or training will be necessary.

I. Company policies and procedures
_____ Employees are punctual
_____ Employees complete required paperwork in a timely fashion
_____ Employees follow prescribed policies and procedures
_____ Employees make well thought-out suggestions for the improvement of policies and procedures
_____ Employees' suggestions about changes in policy or procedure are directed properly, given the existing chain of authority

II. Communication
_____ Employees communicate in a timely fashion
_____ Employees' communication is well thought out
_____ Employees' communication has a point (i.e., it intends to initiate some specific action)
_____ Employees' communication addresses or bears upon its stated intention
_____ Employees direct communication appropriately, given the chain of command and lines of authority
A. Verbal
_____ Employees are articulate
_____ Employees use language that is easily understood
_____ Employees allow the listener to understand both why the communication is necessary and in what actions the communication is supposed to result
_____ Employees limit nonwork-related talk
B. Written
_____ Employees write clearly, in a way that is easily understood
_____ Employees understand the basic elements of style
_____ Employees' writing comes to the point, rather than rambles excessively
C. Listening
_____ Employees exhibit critical listening skills
_____ Employees' listenening skills are as good as their speaking skills
_____ Employees listen to inform themselves

III. Customer service
_____ Employees take the initiative to help customers get what they need
_____ Employees ask questions to clarify what it is the customer wants
_____ Employees give the same level of service to all customers
_____ Employees follow up on customer queries and suggestions
_____ When necessary, employees route customers to those departments and individuals best suited to help them

IV. On-the-job learning
_____ Employees learn new tasks and routines easily
_____ Employees demonstrate an ability to learn from everyone who trains (i.e., they do not have built-in resistances to learning from certain individuals or certain types of people)
_____ Employees are competent to train others in on-the-job tasks
_____ Employees can provide training to everyone, without bias

V. Routine tasks

____ Employees complete routine tasks in the amount of time expected

____ Employees can explain what they do and why they do it

____ Employees can train others to perform routine tasks

____ Employees make well thought out suggestions for the improvement of set routines

SELECTED BIBLIOGRAPHY

Flamholtz, Eric G, Yvonne Randle, and Sonja Sackmann. "Personnel Management: The Tone of Tomorrow." In *Managing People: The Art and Science of Business Management,* vol. 6, ed. by A. Dale Timpe. New York: Facts On File, 1988.

Giesecke, Joan, ed. *Practical Help for New Supervisors.* 3rd ed. Chicago: ALA, 1997.

Green, Thad B. *Motivation Management: Fueling Performance by Discovering What People Believe About Themselves and Their Organizations.* Palo Alto, Calif.: Davies-Black Pub., 2000.

Mayo, Diane, and Jeanne Goodrich. *Staffing for Results: A Guide to Working Smarter.* Chicago: ALA, 2002.

Timpe, A. Dale, ed. *Managing People: The Art and Science of Business Management,* vol. 6. New York: Facts On File, 1988.

Trumfio, Ginger, and William Keenan, Jr. "Managing Strengths for Sales Success." *Sales & Marketing Management* 146, no. 10 (Oct. 1994): 43.

Notes

Team Concepts

FRAN KREMPASKY
Acquisitions/Serials Librarian
Thomas M. Cooley Law School

Creating and managing successful departmental teams and cross-functional teams is often a difficult task for any manager, but especially for technical services managers. Technical service work can be very detail-oriented and focused on procedures. Technical services jobs often require high problem-solving abilities, judgment calls, and the ability work in complex organizations.

This checklist will be of use in establishing or working with any type of team, including special project teams, departmental teams, and work teams. You can help teams be productive by creating measurable goals and deadlines for decision-making. Members of the team working toward meeting mutually accepted goals will avoid a lack of agreement and resistance among the team members to move forward on work tasks and projects.

The team leader needs to put an enabling structure in place that facilitates teamwork and operates within an overall supportive organizational context. The team leader also will need to learn, and even be coached on, how to lead teams effectively.

I. **Formation and arrangement of teams**
   A. Skills assessment: Determine what skills are needed to accomplish the work and which people in the organization have the right skills .
      ____ Technical and functional skills
      ____ Interpersonal skills
      ____ Problem-solving skills
      ____ Organizational skills
   B. Accountability
      ____ Mutual accountability among team members
      ____ Individual accountability of each team member
      ____ Accountability to administration
      ____ Accountability to affected stakeholders outside technical services

C. Commitment
_____ The mission and purpose of the team is clear and understandable
    _____ Each team member understands and shares in the goals
    _____ Performance goals are explicit
        _____ They are realistic
        _____ They are attainable
        _____ They are challenging
    _____ The purpose of the team is meaningful to each member
_____ Staff realize they need to be a team to succeed
_____ There is commitment to the aims and purposes of the team
_____ The leader supports members of the team
_____ The team members support each other
_____ The team leader represents the team
_____ The team leader is the link to the rest of the organization

II. **Attributes of successful teams**
  A. Appropriate leadership
    _____ The leader has skills to develop a team approach
    _____ The leader allocates time to the team and its activities
    _____ Team management is shared because everyone on the team can be a leader
    _____ The team leader must have conflict resolution skills
  B. Suitable membership
    _____ Each member is qualified
    _____ Each team member has a role and performs real and worthwhile work
    _____ A complementary set of skills and needed characteristics are available
    _____ Individual members will need to depend on each other's input to perform their own work
    _____ The team has five to eight people
        _____ Just enough people to do the job and no more
        _____ Small enough group to communicate and convene meetings
        _____ Small enough group to understand roles and responsibilities
  C. Constructive climate
    _____ Support from library administrators
    _____ Support from stakeholders outside technical services
    _____ The perceived need for the project is accepted as a real need within technical services
  D. Desire to achieve
    _____ Be sure the team is clear about objectives
    _____ Set performance targets and goals
        _____ Determine to be achievable
        _____ Set deadlines
    _____ Send progress reports
        _____ To team members
        _____ To administration
    _____ Devote energy primarily to achievement results
    _____ Evaluate performance
    _____ Evaluate processes and team for improvement

III. **Team development**
  A. Clarify roles of team members
    _____ Distinct role of the team within the organization
    _____ Defined individual roles

____ Cross-functional teams
 ____ Make sure job descriptions are available for cross-functions
  ____ Consider whether current job descriptions need modification
  ____ Determine if cross-functional work is included in individual job descriptions
 ____ Determine if new work is recognized
 ____ Consider reassessing pay structure
 ____ Determine priorities between jobs
  ____ Consider shifting priorities
  ____ Decide if some priorities are more important than others
 ____ Include supervisors from both areas (dual evaluation) in job evaluations
____ Confirm appropriate work if jobs fall under union guidelines
____ Clarify communication channels
 ____ Schedule staff meetings regularly
 ____ Develop communication patterns and procedures
____ Make sure administrative procedures are in place to support the team

B. Develop effective work methods
____ Institute procedures for team training
____ Decide if individual staff need training for use of required tools, expertise, knowledge, and skills
____ Document processes and tasks for individuals
____ Put in place a method for problem solving

IV. Facilitator roles and responsibilities
____ Contribute to the structure of the team
____ Clarify main purposes, goals, and objectives of the team
____ Create a positive climate
____ Record key team decisions and discussions
____ Provide resources as needed
____ Coordinate work activities and team tasks
____ Make available the tools and techniques needed to advance work groups
____ Monitor group dynamics
 ____ Assure full participation of group members
 ____ Manage conflicts and differences within the group
____ Provide feedback to the group
____ Make group adjustments
____ Support the group
____ Support individual members of the group
____ Provide coaching as needed
____ Provide necessary technical and procedural training
____ Create job descriptions for each major library function (acquisitions, cataloging, etc.) so when cross-training is required, each team member (and manager) understands the scope and activities associated with the job
____ Have group members understand that they may have a variety of roles that may be changeable

V. Monitoring and assessing team effectiveness and efficiencies
A. Progress reports
____ For team members
____ To administration
 ____ Record key milestones and achievements

     ____ Determine future projects

     ____ List key issues and problems

        ____ Those that have been resolved

        ____ Those that need to be resolved

   ____ Key decisions

     ____ List those already made

     ____ List those that need to be made

        ____ Choose who will make key decisions

        ____ Pick deadlines for decisions to be made

  B. Budget status

     ____ Accommodate any change in objectives

     ____ Accommodate any change in timelines and delivery dates

     ____ Accommodate any change in scope, staff, or financial situation

     ____ Request monies for staff training (especially if creating cross-functional teams)

  C. Next steps

     ____ Help move team forward

     ____ Document what the next steps will be

        ____ Choose who is responsible for meeting the next steps

        ____ Decide on a deadline for the next steps

VI. Outcomes of successful teams

     ____ End product is better than anyone envisioned

     ____ Increased responsibility to each team member and the organization

     ____ Improved communication

     ____ Improved collaboration

SELECTED BIBLIOGRAPHY

Bazirjian, Rosann, and Rebecca Mugridge. *Teams in Library Technical Services.* Lanham, Md.: Scarecrow Press, 2006.

Beatty, Carol A., and Brenda A. Barker Scott. *Building Smart Teams: A Roadmap to High Performance.* Thousand Oaks, Calif.: Sage, 2004.

Bernfeld, Betsy A. "Developing a Team Management Structure in a Public Library." *Library Trends* 53, no.1 (Summer 2004): 112–28.

Beyerlein, Michael M. et al., eds. *The Collaborative Work Systems Fieldbook: Strategies, Tools, and Techniques.* Collaborative Work Systems Series. San Francisco, Calif.: Jossey-Bass, 2003.

Creating Teams with an Edge: The Complete Skill Set to Build Powerful and Influential Reams. The Harvard Business Essentials Series. Boston, Mass.: Harvard Business School Pr., 2004.

Harvey, Thomas R., and Bonita Brolet. *Building Teams, Building People: Expanding the Fifth Resource.* 2nd ed. Lanham, Md.: ScarecrowEducation, 2004.

Katzenback, Jon R., and Douglas K. Smith. *The Wisdom of Teams: Creating High-performance Organization.* New York: HarperBusiness Essentials, 2003.

Lubans, John Jr. "Teams in Libraries." *Library Administration & Management* 17, no. 3 (Summer 2003): 144–46.

Osa, Justina O. "The Dual Nature of Staffing in the Education Library: Management Issues and Solutions." *Education Libraries* 26, no. 2 (Winter 2003): 19–29.

Perry, Valerie E. "Cross-functional Training: A Staff Exchange Program at the University of Kentucky." *Kentucky Libraries* 62, no. 4 (Fall 1998): 3–5.

Training

FRAN KREMPASKY
Acquisitions/Serials Librarian
Thomas M. Cooley Law School

Training is the systematic acquisition of skills, rules, concepts, or attitudes that result in satisfactory or an improved performance. It is a learning activity intended to enhance the ability of a worker to perform or manage current job-related duties and to prepare for future ones.

In the twenty-first century library, where technology is paramount in the delivery and access of library services and resources, training of all library staff members is necessary for the efficient, accurate, and timely preparation and processing of resources. You must analyze the work environment and staff skill levels to determine the necessary training needed for staff. Ultimately, you are responsible for meeting administrative and departmental missions and goals; one way to meet those goals is through staff training.

Training can foster more creative, energetic, and knowledgeable staff, especially if a commitment is made not only to train new individual staff members, but also existing staff. Ongoing training aids in staff retention, enhances previous knowledge and training, and develops staff skills. Personnel at all levels should have the basic skill sets to help them effectively perform their jobs and reduce known gaps in knowledge or skills.

I. **Administrative support**
_____ Develop an administrative plan for staff training
_____ Develop sustainable budget lines for staff training and education
     _____ Library administrative level
     _____ Departmental level
_____ Develop a budget line for new training materials when software and equipment are upgraded
_____ Within the organization, communicate an administrative commitment to staff training and development
     _____ Include training in library goals and mission statements
     _____ Include training in departmental and individual goals statements

II. Staff support

____ Communicate training plans to staff

____ Include ongoing training items in annual evaluations when developing job related goals

III. Training objectives

____ All staff and leadership need to be clear about:

     ____ Objective of training

     ____ Content of training

     ____ Key activities of training

     ____ Skills to be acquired

____ Determine the types of training needed to perform a job or task

____ Leaders and staff need open communication about objectives, priorities, and competencies required for the job

____ Training objectives must support the organization's missions and goals

____ Outcomes of training must be measurable

IV. Establish a plan for training

____ Perform a training needs assessment of all staff

     ____ Relate training needs to department mission and goals

     ____ Examine existing data about current jobs and roles

         ____ Analyze job descriptions

         ____ Analyze grade or job levels

         ____ Observe job tasks being performed

         ____ Question and interview staff about the tasks and jobs they actually perform

     ____ Examine current administrative priorities and projects

     ____ Training must be current and relevant to staff

____ Decide if training will be organizational (include the entire staff), a segment of the staff, or individually based

____ Determine the specific set of staff skills needed

     ____ Identify core competencies or skill sets

         ____ Assess current staff skills

         ____ Examine what kind of training has been requested

         ____ Determine which skill sets have been used previously

         ____ Predict which skills will be needed in the future

     ____ Identify knowledge and education required for the job

____ Evaluate current training documentation

____ Analyze, design, or revise existing training materials and documentation

     ____ To meet professional competencies

     ____ To meet specific skills

         ____ Equipment (e.g., telephones, copiers, printers, and scanners)

         ____ Technology

         ____ OPAC

     ____ To perform specific tasks and jobs

         ____ Order of execution of steps in a task

         ____ Flow-charts

____ Write objectives for job tasks (e.g., "Employee will become familiar with OCLC")

     ____ Determine an action plan

     ____ Determine the successful outcome of the training (e.g., satisfactory completion of tasks)

_____ Determine the delivery method for training. The delivery method must match learning objectives
      _____ The manager or supervisor
      _____ Workshop training (offsite or onsite) for specific skill sets
      _____ In-house training using current trainers or staff or outside trainers
            _____ Collaborative training
            _____ Mentoring and coaching
      _____ "Train-the-trainer"
      _____ Distance or Web training courses
      _____ Conferences
      _____ Continuing Education Unit Credits (CEU's) coursework
      _____ Library consortia or network workshops and courses
      _____ Commercial training company
      _____ Self directed study

V. **Schedule training**
    _____ Take care of logistics
      _____ Select and set up scheduling details
            _____ Location of training
            _____ Dates
            _____ Times
      _____ Determine the content of the class
      _____ Determine the types of training equipment or resources needed
      _____ Set up technology and software needed. Make sure it is useable
      _____ Develop handouts and written evaluations
      _____ Set up travel requirements
      _____ Verify costs and funding
    _____ Establish a clear timeline and schedule for the training plan
      _____ Agenda
      _____ Timeframes and target dates for training period

VI. **Assessment and evaluation of training**
    _____ Determine the successful, measurable outcomes of a training program
      _____ Provide written tests and evaluations
            _____ Measure overall effectiveness
            _____ Learn what was successful, less than successful, or missed in training
    _____ Decide if training continues to meet the goals and mission of the department and administration

VII. **Retraining staff**
    _____ Upgrades to technology and software
    _____ New technology
    _____ Revisions to national standards (e.g., MARC formats, cataloging rules)

VIII. **Training for new technical services staff members**
    _____ Establish local core competencies or best practices
      _____ According to the job description or job title
      _____ According to union policies
    _____ Develop a training schedule the first day or week of work
    _____ Document all procedures
      _____ Update and revise procedures and policies as needed
      _____ Standards must be up-to-date

_____ Train with local workflow, procedures, policies, and practices documentation
  _____ Determine a training schedule
  _____ Determine a list of trainers
  _____ Determine the location of training
  _____ Determine and communicate how the individual will be evaluated on training
  _____ Determine the resource person available to answer questions
  _____ During training, answer questions, follow up with questions, check work, provide feedback, and evaluate work
  _____ Check for any cross-training opportunities
_____ Local information technology and system network training procedures
  _____ Local computer training
  _____ Local operating system training
  _____ Local OPAC training, including module training
  _____ Printers
  _____ FTP
  _____ HTML and XML
  _____ Digital technologies
  _____ Local e-mail system
  _____ Internet and intranet
_____ Training for national library standards, practices, and tools
  _____ OCLC training
  _____ MARC format standards
    _____ Classification
    _____ Bibliographic
    _____ Authority
    _____ Holdings
    _____ Community information
  _____ Metadata standards (e.g., Dublin Core, Text Encoding Initiative [TEI])
  _____ Cataloguing rules (e.g., Anglo-American Cataloging Rules 2, rev. ed. [AACR2r], Resource Description and Access [RDA])
  _____ Subject analysis tools
    _____ Library of Congress Subject Headings (LCSH)
    _____ Sears Subject Headings
    _____ Medical Subject Headings (MeSH)
    _____ Subject thesauri (e.g., Guidelines on Subject Access to Individual Works of Fiction, Drama, etc. [GSAFD], Art and Architecture Thesaurus [AAT])
_____ Classification tools
  _____ Library of Congress Classification Web
  _____ Library of Congress Classification schedules
  _____ OCLC's WebDewey
  _____ Dewey Decimal Classification
_____ Authority tools
  _____ NACO/SACO manual
_____ Vendor tools
  _____ Online research databases
  _____ Online documentation
    _____ Library of Congress
    _____ OCLC
    _____ Local system
  _____ Serials vendors and reports

____ Processing tools
    ____ Labels and label printing
    ____ Barcodes
    ____ Bindery software

SELECTED BIBLIOGRAPHY

Anthony, Betsy. "The University of Virginia Library Staff Education and Development Program and Vision for the Library of Tomorrow." *Education Libraries* 23, no. 2–3 (1999): 9–18.

Avery, Elizabeth Fuseler, Terry Dahlin, and Deborah A. Carver. *Staff Development: A Practical Guide.* 3rd ed. Chicago: ALA, 2001.

Branton, Ann. "Guidelines for Supervising and Managing a Cataloging Department." *Mississippi Libraries* 67, no. 1 (Spring 2003): 16–18.

Giesecke, Joan, and Beth McNeil. "Core Competencies and the Learning Organization." *Library Administration and Management* 13, no. 3 (Summer 1999): 158–66.

Letarte, Karen M., Michelle R. Turvey, Dea Borneman, and David L. Adams. "Practitioner Perspectives on Cataloging Education for Entry-level Academic Librarians." *Library Resources & Technical Services* 46, no. 1 (Jan. 2002): 11–22.

Lynch, Beverly P., and Kimberley Robles Smith. "The Changing Nature of Work in Academic Libraries." *College & Research Libraries* 62, no. 5 (Spring 2001): 407–20.

Massis, Bruce E. *The Practical Library Manager.* New York: Haworth Pr., 2003.

Naylor, Richard J. "Core Competencies: What They Are and How to Use Them." *Public Libraries* 39, no. 2 (Mar./Apr. 2000): 108–14.

Wilkie, Katerine, and Roger Strouse. *Custom Report Prepared for OCLC Institute: OCLC Library Training and Education Market Needs Assessment Study.* Burlingame, Calif.: Outsell, 2003.

Notes

ART OF MANAGEMENT

Management Styles

FRAN KREMPASKY
Acquisitions/Serials Librarian
Thomas M. Cooley Law School

Y ou practice various management and leadership styles with your employees, taking into account your own personal style, your organizational setting, and union practices, as well as incorporating the values and missions of your own department and those of the organization. The many concepts and theories developed on management styles emanate from the fields of science, psychology, sociology, and anthropology. Because this field is vast and ever-changing, you must read the literature of management theory to get a grasp of how you most-effectively can lead the work of your employees and play a major role in influencing your employees' performances. You also will want to maintain employee job satisfaction and morale within the department, while still attaining organizational goals. Being learned and skilled in leadership theories and practices will help you as a new manager.

The management style or styles selected must fit you as well as the organization. Management styles must be tailored to your organization, taking into account the many complexities in today's working culture and environments. Understanding the variations of management styles—and the pros and cons of each—will help you toward creating a more cooperative and productive environment, whereby you and your employees will be able to meet the goals and missions of your teams successfully.

Workplace management styles and theories are complex and should not be treated as a one-step solution. With this in mind, some of the more popular and key management styles found in library and business management literature are listed below. As a new manager, you must keep in mind that no best leadership style exists, and in the reality of today's work environments, a combination of the styles is preferred. The styles are presented as options and are meant as a tool for further contemplation and research.

I. **Analyze existing management styles and necessary resources**
   A. Administrative support and work environment
       ____ Analyze work and management culture
       ____ Determine organizational goals and missions and find a shared vision
       ____ Notice existing management styles and practices already operating within the organization and determine if they meet goals effectively
           ____ Determine if styles and practices are organizationally mandated

      ____ Consider adopting a variant management style and analyze the organizational support for variant styles

      ____ Find out whether colleagues informally know what styles are rewarded in your organization and which are not, as buy-in from staff above and below is key

  ____ Talk to other supervisors within the organization to find out more information

  ____ Find out if the administration is supportive of a certain type of style

  ____ Determine how much legitimate authority the leader possesses

  ____ Adapt a leadership style of behaviors that meet the needs of the employees, the environment, and the situation

  ____ In implementation and evaluation, always remember that leading and managing teams is a process that is flexible and changeable. As situations, people, and the organization develop, so do styles

B. Analyze staff and employees

  ____ Determine if employees participate in decision-making, as it is crucial for buy-in

  ____ Consider whether employees are ready for change, and analyze their needs, desires, and values

  ____ Determine the employee's commitment, competence, and knowledge of the organization, tasks, etc.

  ____ Find out if employees show a willingness to accept responsibility, as they can be self-directed and creative in their jobs if given the chance

C. Analyze your own management style

  ____ Determine your personal values

  ____ Determine your current style

  ____ Establish your needs and interests

  ____ Figure out your perception of the situation and your employees; consider whether your employees have a low or high tolerance for change or structure

  ____ Evaluate whether you are flexible and adaptable in style, as it is important, especially because work environments and situations will change

  ____ Determine how your team members perceive you as a leader; a favorable or unfavorable perception may suggest a selection of a particular style

II. Styles of leadership and management

A. Types of leaders[1]

  ____ **Visionary:** Moves people toward shared dreams. The leader must be aware of the big picture. The team has shared goals and collective tasks. This style is used when changes require new vision or when clear direction is needed

  ____ **Coaching:** Connects what a person wants with organizational goals. The leader will aid people in identifying their unique strengths and weaknesses, tying them to personal career goals. Helps employees improve performance by building team capabilities. Coaching often helps to boost performance

  ____ **Affiliative:** Creates harmony and connects people in a positive way. Helps strengthen connections on teams. Can be used to motivate staff during stressful times

  ____ **Democratic:** Values people's input and garners commitment through participation. Valuable for building consensus

---

1. Daniel Goleman, Richard Boyatzis, and Annie McKee, *Primal Leadership: Realizing the Power of Emotional Intelligence* (Boston, Mass.: Harvard Business School Pr., 2002.)

_____ **Pacesetting:** A style that attempts to meet challenging and exciting goals. A means to get highly competent team members motivated. However, because so frequently implemented poorly, the results are often very negative. Can also provoke anxiety in employees

_____ **Commanding (Coercive):** Immediate compliance with orders without explaining reasons; requires tight control and monitoring. Soothes fears by giving clear directions in crisis. Because it is often misused, this type can be highly negative. Can be used in a crisis when quick results are needed

B. Management styles (A combination of styles is preferred; cultural, gender, and other factors may affect communication and leadership styles.)

_____ **Situational Leadership:** Generally, situational leadership relies on the assumption that there is no one superior leadership model in all situations. The best leaders are those who are adaptable to various types of people and situations. (Hersey, Blanchard, and Johnson created the situational leadership model for use by managers to help them decide which leadership styles are most appropriate in various situations.[2])

_____ **Consensus Management** (people-oriented): Helps to preserve relationships, is participatory in nature, and is consensual. Human interaction is important. Prefers that everyone involved be satisfied in achieving the goal

_____ **Task-Oriented** (command and control): Leader may be seen as logical, dominant, aggressive, autocratic, independent, competitive, decisive, and task oriented. Concentrates on getting the work done

C. Rensis Likert theory of management styles (Rensis Likert studied human behaviors within organizations and is well known for his work with management systems, especially in industry.[3])

_____ **Authoritative:** Management imposes decisions. The manager is autocratic, and decisions are generated at the top of the organization; fear and punishment are motivators. Communication flows from the top with little teamwork. In the short run, productivity will increase but it will taper off because of negative effects

_____ **Benevolent-Authoritative:** Management is condescending to employees, expects employees to be compliant and mostly motivated by rewards. Decisions mostly made at the top but with some communication with employees. (One of two styles mostly used by libraries.)

_____ **Consultative:** Management has substantial but not complete trust in employees. Managers see motivation as being rewards with some involvement in decision-making. Top management makes most decisions but asks for ideas from employees. Communication flows up and down. (One of two styles mostly used by libraries)

_____ **Participative:** Managers have complete trust and confidence in employees. Group participation is used in decision-making on all levels. Communication flows both up and down and horizontally among peers. Employees are more highly motivated to achieve organizational goals and objectives. Increases job satisfaction but must entail top-level support because conflicts can still arise. Participative management also affords employees a clearer idea of the organization's missions and goals and the implementation strategy

2. Paul Hersey, Kenneth H. Blanchard, and Dewey E. Johnson, _Management of Organizational Behavior: Leading Human Resources,_ 8th ed. (Upper Saddle River, N.J.: Prentice Hall, 2001).

3. Robert D. Stueart and Barbara B. Moran, _Library and Information Center Management,_ 4th ed. (Englewood, Colo.: Libraries Unlimited, 1993).

4. Fred Edward Fiedler and Martin M. Chemers, _Improving Leadership Effectiveness: The Leader Match Concept,_ 2nd ed. (New York: Wiley, 1984).

D. Contingency model theory[4] (Leadership style used is dependent on the situation. Some situations will require employee-centered leadership; production-centered leadership may suit reaching short-term specific goals)

____ In very favorable conditions where the leader has power, informal backing, and a relatively well-structured task, the group is ready to be directed on how to go about accomplishing its task

____ Under very unfavorable conditions, the group will fall apart unless the leader shows active intervention and control to keep workers on task

____ Situational variables: Leadership depends as much on the organizational variables as it does on the leader's own personal leadership attributes

III. Leadership style guidelines and objectives

All staff and leadership need to be clear about:

____ Creating the vision—a picture of what the group should become. This vision needs to be transmitted to others in the organization

____ Developing the team—bring together qualified people who are jointly responsible for achieving the group goal

____ Clarifying values—organizational values must be identified and communicated

____ Positioning—develop effective strategies for moving the group toward the vision

____ Communicating—develop common understanding with others by communicating effectively at all levels

____ Empowering—includes motivating and coaching

____ Measuring—identify critical success factors associated with a group's operation. Used as a way to measure group progress and success

SELECTED BIBLIOGRAPHY

Blanchard, Kenneth H. *Leadership and the One Minute Manager: Increasing Effectiveness through Situational Leadership.* New York: Morrow, 1985.

Fiedler, Fred Edward, and Martin M. Chemers. *Improving Leadership Effectiveness: The Leader Match Concept.* 2nd ed. New York: Wiley, 1984.

Goleman, Daniel, Richard Boyatzis, and Annie McKee. *Primal Leadership: Realizing the Power of Emotional Intelligence.* Boston, Mass.: Harvard Business School Pr., 2002.

Hersey, Paul, Kenneth H. Blanchard, and Dewey E. Johnson. *Management of Organizational Behavior: Leading Human Resources.* 8th ed. Upper Saddle River, N.J.: Prentice Hall, 2001.

Hitt, William D. *The Leader-manager: Guidelines for Action.* Columbus, Ohio: Battelle Press, 1988.

Howze, Philip C. "Perspectives on . . . Collegiality, Collegial Management, and Academic Libraries." *The Journal of Academic Librarianship* 29, no. 1 (January 2003): 40–43.

Kim, Soonhee. "Participative Management and Job Satisfaction: Lessons for Management Leadership." *Public Administration Review* 62, no. 2 (Mar./Apr. 2002): 231–42.

LAMA/LOMS Comparative Library Organization Committee (CLOC) and CLOC Bibliography Task Force. "Required Reading for Library Administrators, Part Two: An Annotated Bibliography of Highly Cited Library and Information Science Authors and Their Works." *Library Administration & Management* 17, no. 1 (Winter 2003): 11–20.

Massis, Bruce E. *The Practical Library Manager.* New York: Haworth Pr., 2003.

Stueart, Robert D., and Barbara B. Moran. *Library and Information Center Management.* 6th ed. Englewood, Colo.: Libraries Unlimited, 2002.

Valentine, Doug. "Gender and Organizational Culture." *Library Administration & Management* 17, no. 3 (Summer 2003): 130–34.

Decision Making

JUNE DEWEESE
Head of Access Services
University of Missouri-Columbia

ANDREA KAPPLER
Cataloging Manager
Evansville Vanderburgh Public Library

Sometimes, decision-making styles are reflective of the culture of an individual library, and sometimes they are varied and diverse within a library system and depend upon the style of the individual leader, but effective decision-making has many of the same elements regardless of the culture or the individual leader. If decision-making is not timely, it is rarely successful. You should not make decisions in a hurry and without thinking of the implications for both the organization as a whole, the persons within the organization, and those served by the organization. Decisions made in haste are often regretted later. To be effective, take both the macro and the micro approach by thinking about who is most affected by the decision, as well as the long- and short-term implications of the decision.

I. **Define the problem and create a timeline for the decision**
    ____ Identify your problem carefully, acknowledging its complexity
        ____ It is a minor problem
        ____ It is a major problem
        ____ Figure out if previous decisions are still workable, and change decisions that are no longer appropriate
    ____ Know when a decision must be made
    ____ Know the consequences if the decision is not made by a specific date or time
    ____ Avoid rushing an important decision just because others expect it

II. **Specify your goals and objectives**
    ____ Ask yourself what you want to accomplish
    ____ Know which of your interests, values, concerns, fears, and aspirations are most relevant to achieving your goal
    ____ Know short- and long-term objectives of:
        ____ Teams and work units
        ____ Department
        ____ Organization

III. **Determine who is affected by the decision (the stakeholders)**
_____ Individual employees
_____ Teams within the department
  _____ Acquisitions and collection development
  _____ Cataloging
  _____ Serials
  _____ Processing
  _____ Other units in your technical services department
_____ Areas and people outside the department
  _____ Computers and IT
  _____ Other departments in the library (i.e., the effect of decisions made in technical services on public services)
  _____ Patrons
_____ Involve the stakeholders
  _____ Ask relevant questions
  _____ Ask for their assistance in doing research on the topic and gathering information
  _____ Ask them to share their experience and expertise on the topic

IV. **Create imaginative alternatives**
_____ Examine every alternative you can think of before making a decision
_____ Consider the implications of each alternative
_____ Evaluate all possible solutions
_____ Ask your team if they support your choice among the alternatives

V. **Understand the consequences**
_____ Immediate consequences
_____ Short-term consequences
_____ Long-term consequences
_____ People who can help you determine the fiscal implications of the decision
_____ Financial implications of the decision
  _____ Costs in terms of staff time
  _____ Costs in terms of materials (spine labels, paper, etc.)
  _____ Costs in terms of money
_____ The decision's ethical, moral, or legal implications
_____ What could go wrong

VI. **Be aware of trade-offs and risks**
_____ List possible effects of any action and how much damage it could inflict
_____ Be aware of proposed trade-offs that endanger the objectives
_____ Keep a list of the trade-offs you are making
_____ Look for external factors that could affect your decision
_____ Never sacrifice the future for the short-term unless there is no option

VII. **Clarify uncertainties**
_____ Focus your research by asking yourself what information you need to make your decision
_____ Gather information, but do not spend too much time researching (the definition of what constitutes "too much time" is based upon local custom and can best be determined in discussion and consultation with experienced staff persons in each institution)

VIII. Make the decision

_____ Make a checklist of the main issues before finalizing any decision

_____ Try to uncover any hidden flaws (potential problems caused by the decision) before finalizing your decision

_____ If approval from higher-level managers is needed, produce a written report or presentation if necessary

    _____ Be prepared to explain the reasons for your decision

    _____ Be prepared to describe the effects of your decision on individuals and departments

    _____ Be open to questioning

    _____ Be willing to make changes in response to genuine objections and concerns

_____ Make sure your decision is well-founded and well-grounded so that changes will not be necessary (however, in a flexible workplace, one must be prepared to change one's mind when new information presents itself and makes a change necessary)

IX. Communicate the decision

_____ Inform all levels within your organization:

    _____ Persons to whom you report

    _____ Colleagues

    _____ Staff

_____ Be as honest as possible when communicating a decision to staff

    _____ Break down your decision into its component parts

    _____ Discuss the key objectives of each part

    _____ Discuss the actions required to complete each objective

    _____ Delegate responsibility for completion of each action

    _____ Share with colleagues a deadline for completing each action

    _____ Agree on points to the progress of each action

_____ Welcome contributions from anybody who will be affected

X. Implement the decision

_____ Develop an action plan to implement the decision

    _____ Decide when to implement the decision

        _____ Choose a date when the decision becomes effective

        _____ Select deadlines for completing each action related to the decision

    _____ Create documentation and information related to the decision and its implementation

_____ Involve others in implementing the decision

    _____ Persons to whom you report

    _____ Colleagues

    _____ Staff

_____ Schedule a meeting with supervisors, colleagues, or employees affected by the decision

    _____ Break down your decision into its component parts

    _____ Discuss the key objectives of each part of the decision

    _____ Explain the actions required to complete each objective

    _____ Delegate responsibility for completion of each action item

    _____ Give colleagues or employees deadlines for completing each action

    _____ Agree on points to monitor the progress of each action

    _____ Allow and encourage colleagues or employees to ask questions relating to the decision or its implementation

    _____ Try to anticipate objections with well-researched information

XI. **Monitor the progress of a decision**
____ Check the progress of a decision at natural breakpoints or specific intervals
____ Be open to modifying your original decision if needed

XII. **Assess the results of a decision**
____ Evaluate whether your decision provided the desired outcome
____ If the decision succeeded, explain how you know it did
____ If the decision failed, explain why it failed
____ Evaluate if the decision gave you lessons from which to learn. If so, record the lessons so they can be absorbed by you or other people in the future

SELECTED BIBLIOGRAPHY

Brewer, Joseph M., Sheril J. Hook, Janice Simmons-Welburn, and Karen Williams. "Libraries Dealing with the Future Now." *Association of Research Libraries* no. 234 (Jun. 2004): 1–9.

Hammond, John S., Ralph L. Keeney, and Howard Raiffa. *Smart Choices: A Practical Guide to Making Better Decisions.* Boston, Mass.: Harvard Business School Pr., 1999.

Heller, Robert. *Making Decisions.* 1st American ed. New York: DK Publishing, 1998.

Osif, Bonnie A. "Leadership." *Library Administration & Management* 18, no. 3 (Summer 2004): 162–66.

Robbins, Stephen P. *Decide & Conquer: Make Winning Decisions and Take Control of Your Life.* Upper Saddle River, N.J.: Financial Times/Prentice Hall, 2004.

Schoaf, Eric C. "New Technologies and Constant Change: Managing the Process." *The Journal of Academic Librarianship* 30, no. 4 (Jul. 2004): 322–27.

Shorb, Stephen R. "Ethical Decision-Making in Library Administration." *The Southeastern Librarian* 52, no. 3 (Fall 2004): 3–8.

Welch, David A. *Decisions, Decisions: The Art of Effective Decision Making.* Amherst, N.Y.: Prometheus Bks., 2002.

Customer Service

STEPHEN COCHRAN

Librarian

Washington State Department of Transportation

Serving customers is at the heart of all library services. Without customers, there is no reason to open the doors, turn on the computers, buy the books and catalog them, or develop programming.

How you serve customers will affect whether they come back, tell their friends, and advocate for the library. Additionally, technical services has both internal and external customers. The timeliness with which you catalog and process materials affects the customers who walk through the door—the external customers. The effectiveness of your acquisitions strategy and the quality and consistency of your reporting to collection development staff about things such as cancellations, back orders, and price changes affects the staff to whom you deliver the goods everyday—the internal customers.

These internal customers (e.g., public services staff) rely on technical services on a daily basis, and poor service to them will often get passed along as poor service to library customers. If acquisitions does not have this summer's hot title in adequate quantities, cataloged and ready for checkout, and in the library on the book's release date, then the adult services staff ends up looking unprofessional, and they will resent it. If materials for reserve are not rush ordered and always at the top of the cataloging queue, the circulation and reserve staff continually have to tell anxious students the title is not yet available.

I. **The FISH! Service Philosophy lists four simple and interrelated concepts that are a recipe for exceptional customer service[1]:**

     ____ **Play!** Those who think that play is the opposite of work are mistaken. Those who take a playful attitude towards their tasks achieve some of the most productive and error-free work. Play releases and energizes the creativity and problem-solving abilities within us, makes really boring work more tolerable, and helps the time fly by. Playing with and having fun with your customers allows them to have fun too, makes them happier, and is a sure fire way to . . .

---

1. Stephen C. Lundin, *Fish!: A Remarkable Way to Boost Morale and Improve Results* (New York: Hyperion, 2000).

_____ **Make their day!** If you do something—anything positive, really—to make the library experience stick out in people's minds, then you have "made their day." Letting kids scan their own barcodes at checkout usually makes their day. Sometimes just remembering particular habits or vices of customers will make their day. When customers see you having fun at your job, your spirit becomes contagious, and they want to join in. Look at difficult people as a challenge—a game, even. It is easier to make people's day if they are already in good spirits. But if they are being difficult, you get a chance to really prove yourself. React to each person as an individual. Ask yourself, "What would make this person's day? What can I do?" Pay attention to them:

_____ **Be there!** Have you ever been out to lunch and stopped at a restaurant where the staff was also out to lunch? What was your reaction? Have you ever gone up to a counter and had the service person deal with you while making a phone call, taking care of personal hygiene, or talking to another worker? What impact did that have on you? Those people were not *being there* in that moment, with you, and it had an impact. If you act like this at work, you are not playing anything but solitaire, and you certainly will not make the customer's day. Many people notice that their first couple of weeks at a new job is really productive. It is because they have to *be there!* Nothing is routine! Then, when it becomes routine, they can space out and have that out-of-body experience called work. Being there is hard and takes practice. You have to know how to catch yourself not being there, and bring yourself back. You have to strive every day to focus, listen, hear, look, and keep your mind and yourself there. This means first and foremost that you have to . . .

_____ **Choose your attitude!** This last point of the FISH! philosophy is really the foundation upon which the other three rest. To have the FISH! attitude and *consistently* live and work by the first three points, you have to recognize that, whether you want to or not, you choose your attitude. Certainly there are customers who can be abusive, but you choose to let it get under your skin. "Leave me alone, I am having a bad day" is something you *decide* you are having and about which you are not going to do anything except try to spread the negativity around

II. **Rick Tate and Gary M. Heil outline a number of very useful concepts that will improve an organization's customer service[2]**

_____ **Make a commitment to service.** You must be committed to serving everyone who comes through the door. Do not just try to satisfy the customer; consistently work to exceed the expectations that customers have. Try to make their day by giving them a memorable experience, one that they will want to try and repeat

_____ **Search out—and satisfy—disgruntled customers.** You will not be able to improve service if you do not know that people are dissatisfied with things you do. Ask often "What could I have done to make your experience more pleasant?" and work every day toward addressing the answers you receive

_____ **Institute a continuous improvement strategy.** Real improvement in service is the cumulative result of many tiny improvements, made daily, at every level in the organization, because no one accepts the status quo, and everyone is committed to change and continuous improvement

_____ **Listen to customers.** This is all about *being there*

_____ **Facilitate change.** Bad service is usually the result of bad leadership: those in positions of leadership who refuse to allow change or who will not update outmoded

---

2. Rick Tate and Gary M. Heil, "Ten Steps to Improved Service," Speakers Platform www.speaking.com/articles_html/RickTateandGaryM.Heil_215.html (accessed Feb. 10, 2006).

structures, policies, and ways of doing things. Being a change agent is a huge part of implementing a continuous improvement strategy

_____ **Define the playing field.** If you do not know what is allowed and what is not, customers end up being told such things as, "I would like to help you but it is not my job," "I only follow policy, I do not write it." These responses are the consequence of a risky service culture created by inflexible policies and inconsistent goals and objectives

_____ **Promote autonomy.** Creative, happy, and positive employees who routinely make business decisions and improvise when necessary are the foundation of excellent service. Libraries often ignore the benefits of engaging their work force's talents and instead ask frontline employees to park their brains at the door and blindly obey predetermined policies and procedures

_____ **Measure performance.** If the work you and your employees do cannot be measured empirically and objectively, then no standard exists to gauge the performance of your library against another or to gauge whether a particular employee's work has improved at all. Workload analysis and process analysis is essential not only for the manager who is evaluating staff, but for the staff themselves.[3] For instance, workload analysis might be used to validate staff members who complain they are overworked. Continuous improvement is nothing but a catchphrase if you cannot answer the question: "Improved as compared to what?"

_____ **Celebrate success.** Even as they strive to improve and know that they can always do better, libraries and library departments that meet their performance goals and objectives should celebrate and be celebrated. Recognition of a job well done should be as ongoing as the desire to improve

SELECTED BIBLIOGRAPHY

Hernon, Peter. *Assessing Service Quality: Satisfying the Expectations of Library Customers.* Chicago: ALA, 1998.
Lundin, Stephen C. *Fish!: A Remarkable Way to Boost Morale and Improve Results.* New York: Hyperion, 2000.
Mayo, Diane, and Jeanne Goodrich. *Staffing for Results: A Guide to Working Smarter.* Chicago: ALA, 2002.
Tate, Rick, and Gary M. Heil. "Ten Steps to Improved Service." Speakers Platform. www.speaking.com/articles_html/RickTateandGaryM.Heil_215.html (accessed May 3, 2007).

3. Diane Mayo and Jeanne Goodrich, *Staffing for Results: A Guide to Working Smarter* (Chicago: ALA, 2002).

Notes

COMMUNICATION

Guidelines for Effective Communication

STEPHEN COCHRAN
Librarian
Washington State Department of Transportation

ALTHEA ASCHMAN
Head of Cataloging
Virginia Tech University

Communication has four main components, each of which, for ease of understanding, is associated with an organ:

1. the conscious translation of an idea or mental construct into language (brain);
2. the transmission of this language to another person or persons (mouth);
3. the receipt of the language by another person or persons (ear); and
4. the conscious translation of the language back into an idea or mental construct by those who have just received it (brain)

It is easy to see—given the amount of translation and decoding required—why so much *miscommunication* takes place. Nevertheless, communication is at the heart of what supervisors do. Having and using effective communication skills will make the difference between being a supervisor and being a *great* supervisor.

For all the advances that have been made in information storage, transmission, and retrieval, there are still primarily two ways for communication to take place between one person and one or more other persons: spoken communication and written communication. Much of what gets missed in business communication is proper attention to step 3, as explained previously.

I. **Effective listening**
    _____ Consider if you are explaining too much and not inquiring enough
    _____ Determine if people respond to what you say without listening (regurgitating their preconceived notions and prejudices without really internalizing new information)
    _____ Actively encourage listening by being a listener

II. **Effective communicating**
    _____ The more predictable the message is, the less information it contains
    _____ Each communication should have new information

_____ Dialogue is about a shared inquiry, a way of thinking and reflecting together

_____ Dialogue is not something you do *to* another person but *with* people

III. **Written communication**

    A. Types

        _____ Letters

        _____ E-mail

        _____ Memos

        _____ Notes

        _____ Advertisements and announcements

        _____ Press releases and public service announcements

        _____ Instant messaging

        _____ Chat rooms

        _____ Weblogs (blogs)

        _____ Really Simple Syndication (RSS) feeds

        _____ Marginalia

    B. When to use written communication

        _____ For information that needs to be retained and critically analyzed

        _____ For information that, over time, requires you not only to transfer but to refine

        _____ For situations in which you require critical feedback

        _____ In circumstances where you have more than one point of information you wish to share

        _____ For occasions in which documentation is important

            _____ Personnel matters

            _____ Long-term projects

        _____ In cases where information you share requires others to funnel information back to you

        _____ When you require work or research to answer questions you raise

        _____ In situations where specific persons will be held accountable for providing specific answers

        _____ When the success or failure of people to provide you with feedback, answers, and critical analysis will impact performance evaluations

IV. **Spoken communication**

    More information can be exchanged in a given length of time via spoken communication

    A. Types

        _____ Face to face or one-on-one

        _____ Speeches

        _____ Intercom

        _____ Voicemail

        _____ Group meetings

        _____ Press conferences

    B. When to use spoken communication

        _____ When you need a yes or no answer with no justification

        _____ In cases where a short answer to a routine operational or procedural matter will suffice

        _____ In situations in which you have only one piece of information to share

        _____ When the communication is anecdotal or personal

        _____ When you seek very-short term help (ten minutes to a half-hour) on an issue

V. **Communication dimensions**
   A. Verbal (uses words)
      ____ Speaking
      ____ Writing
      ____ Word choices
   B. Nonverbal
      ____ Actions
      ____ Body language
      ____ Facial expressions and mannerisms
   C. Cultural influences
      ____ Societal
      ____ Ethnic
      ____ Organizational culture ("How we do things here")

VI. **Listening**
      ____ Pay full attention to the speaker
      ____ Work hard at listening
      ____ Paraphrase the content
      ____ Check out your inferences
      ____ Empathize
      ____ Work on remembering the message

VII. **Perception**
      ____ Be aware that supervisors and subordinates may interpret work problems substantially differently
      ____ Develop awareness of effects of differing perceptions on receiving and understanding messages
      ____ Guard against selective perception that could cause you to miss important cues

SELECTED BIBLIOGRAPHY

Baker, Kim. *How to Say It Online: Everything You Need to Know to Master the New Language of Cyberspace.* Paramus, N.J.: Prentice Hall, 2001.

DiZazzo, Raymond. *Saying the Right Thing: A Business Parable.* Naperville, Ill: Sourcebooks, 1997.

Isaacs, William. *Dialogue and the Art of Thinking Together.* New York: Currency, 1999.

Jeary, Tony. *Life is a Series of Presentations: Eight Ways to Punch up Your People Skills at Work, at Home, Anytime, Anywhere.* New York: Fireside Bks., 2004.

Toogood, Granville N. *The Articulate Executive: Learn to Look, Act, and Sound Like a Leader.* New York: McGraw-Hill, 1996.

Von Neumann, John, and Oskar Morgenster. *Theory of Games and Economic Behavior.* Princeton, N.J.: Princeton Univ. Pr., 1944.

Notes

Communicating Up, Down, and Sideways

ALTHEA ASCHMAN
Head of Cataloging
Virginia Tech University

As a manager, you generally answer to one or more people above you in the hierarchy. The first-time supervisor should spend the first month of the job ascertaining what the boss wants and concentrating on how to provide it. The care and feeding of the relationship between you and your boss is of utmost importance and requires constant cultivation and maintenance.

As a supervisor you will have personnel who answer to you. You need to be able to give clear directions and guidance to these employees as well as providing needed resources for them to do their jobs and achieve desired results. You will need to communicate important information from the people above you to your staff.

The third set of people with whom you need to work is your peer group—other supervisors at the same level in the library. Knowing how information flows in your organization is important and knowing the proper channels when making requests, reporting information, and the like will save you much grief. Violating these protocols can lead to much mental angst. It behooves a manager to become politically savvy.

GENERAL

I. **Contexts of organizational communication**
_____ Interpersonal dyad (one-to-one)
_____ Group communication among several people
_____ Public communication: from one to many
_____ Communication between units within technical services
_____ Interdepartmental communication
_____ From organization to organization (external communication)

II. **Going through channels**
_____ Find out what the channels actually are

_____ Realize that you incur risk when you violate the protocol for going through channels

_____ Avoid surprising people

III. **Validate people in the organization (especially important for subordinates)**

    _____ Recognize people when what they do is valuable and valued, regardless of your position

    _____ Speak positively about the organization

    _____ Avoid devaluing people whose points of view differ from yours or whose behavior offends you. Instead find out about their reasoning

IV. **Organizational structure in relation to communication flow**

    A. Hierarchical or tall structure

        _____ You need to know to whom to talk about which topics and understand the chain of command

        _____ Communication flows from top down

        _____ Communication is restricted from the bottom up

        _____ Distortion of messages increases with the number of levels through which they pass

        _____ In the chain-of-command model, you interact with direct reports and with your immediate supervisor, and communication should flow through every link in the chain

    B. Flat structure

        _____ The few hierarchical levels are loose in terms of control and supervision, with more people reporting to a single supervisor

        _____ Individual job autonomy is necessary and empowering, but it can lead to neglect of communication. Prevent such neglect by being attentive to the communication needs of the unit

        _____ Communication problems can result in information overload and loss of control

        _____ Increased span of control and decreased role specialization can exacerbate ambiguity regarding what to communicate and to whom, as well as causing decreased task efficiency

        _____ Ensuring that the communication needs of the unit and the organization are met requires extra vigilance

        _____ You play an important role in providing information to reporting personnel and relaying information from subordinates to bosses

    C. Informal network (the grapevine)

        _____ Beware of the grapevine and use it with great caution to get and give information

        _____ Know who the opinion leaders are. This cannot be determined by position alone

        _____ Feed information into the network using opinion leaders

        _____ Carefully evaluate information received through informal channels, consider the sources, and compare it to official information

        _____ Take advantage of opportunities for conversation by the water cooler and use them wisely

        _____ Be aware that with whom you socialize on the job will be noticed

COMMUNICATION WITH SUBORDINATES

V. **Functions of supervisor in regards to employee communication**

    _____ Information transfer and exchange

    _____ Instruction and direction

    _____ Influence and persuasion

_____ Integration, inclusion, and maintenance
      _____ Keeping the organization operating
      _____ Going through proper channels
      _____ Sorting, disseminating, and explaining data or research results
      _____ Integrating parts of a process or the organization into the whole
      _____ Validation of self, employees, and organization
_____ Conflict management
_____ Giving presentations
_____ Leading meetings
_____ Training
_____ Decisions
      _____ If you or someone above you has already made a decision, tell employees what the decision is in clear language
      _____ When you ask for group input for help with a decision, tell the group how it will be used
            _____ You will make the decision and give consideration to the input given
            _____ The group will make the decision
                  _____ Majority rule
                  _____ Consensus

VI. Build bridges to nurture relationships with the people you count on to get the work done
    _____ Foster two-way communication and personal exchanges
    _____ Expect everyone to display common courtesy and appropriate social behavior
    _____ Demonstrate caring and genuine interest in employees
    _____ Do not make social exchanges contingent on performance needs alone
    _____ Have empathy for others' needs and goals
    _____ Engage in ongoing, joint problem-solving and conflict-resolution activities
    _____ Display lightheartedness and fun, with minimal sarcasm and negative attitudes
    _____ Avoid dominating conversations
    _____ Identify and resolve problems that interfere with optimal communication or performance
    _____ Keep your word and your end of a bargain
    _____ Never make a promise you cannot keep

VII. Communicate leadership worthy of trust
    _____ Effective communication is the glue that holds together working relationships
    _____ Your word is truthful, you say what you mean, and you mean what you say
    _____ Everyone must be treated with dignity and respect, as you would like to be treated
    _____ Employees should be able to trust you with anything

VIII. Establish open, ongoing, and focused two-way communication
    _____ Develop the skills to meet people's critically important communication needs
    _____ Provide employees with the information they need to do their work efficiently and effectively
    _____ Assess the communication needs
      _____ Job related
      _____ Organization-related
      _____ Importance of information—determine "need to know" or "nice to know"
    _____ Determine what vehicles are most appropriate for communicating in a particular situation

_____ Determine how often is it necessary to communicate about any particular issue or with any particular individual

_____ Inform employees about events and developments taking place in the organization that might affect their futures

_____ Provide a vehicle through which employees may be heard

_____ Develop an ongoing and systematic communication process, rather than helter-skelter and crisis driven

_____ Be sure you are not the cause of any of these communication effectiveness compromisers:

     _____ Moving too fast, without allowing time for communication and assimilation

     _____ Information and data overload

     _____ Merely sharing information and data, without the context or sure understanding of the message

     _____ Allowing the abundance of technologies for communicating that can lose the personal touch and dehumanize communication

     _____ Failing to articulate ideas or state succinctly what you want

COMMUNICATING UP AND DOWN

IX. Taking and giving credit

_____ Reward people for knowledge, learning, development, and the sharing of all these things, especially because the assignment of credit for knowledge-based activities is an increasingly important managerial issue in all organizations

_____ Give credit where credit is due; do not steal credit

_____ Recognize conflation of ideas and give credit to the initiators

_____ Recognize competition for recognition among employees

_____ If your boss does something that benefits you or contributes to your success, acknowledge it (publicly if appropriate)

UPWARD COMMUNICATION

X. Communicating with your boss

_____ Identify what motivates your boss

_____ Observe your boss when he or she is unmotivated and record any contributing factors you notice

_____ Learn your boss's dislikes and develop strategies for avoiding or working around them

_____ Figure out what your boss wants from you and make it your business to provide it

_____ Clarify expectations if you need to

_____ Identify, accept, and deal with your boss's style

     _____ Dominant, controlling

     _____ Influencing, charismatic

     _____ Steady, plodding

     _____ Conforming

_____ Prepare for when you are asking something of your supervisor, and take the time to articulate yourself clearly and succinctly

     _____ Questions

     _____ Requests for information

         _____ Be able to justify the benefit to the organization of your having the information

         _____ Know how it will help you do your job

_____ Requests for something, such as equipment, resources
_____ Prepare for when you are telling your supervisor and sharing information
_____ Choose what information to share
_____ Assess appropriateness
_____ Discern what level of detail to provide
_____ Keep the boss informed and give progress reports

REFINING YOURSELF

XI. **Manage speech, silence, and disclosure**
_____ Know when to be circumspect, when to talk, and how much to share
_____ Use care with confidential and proprietary information
_____ Never betray a confidence
_____ Deflect gossip
_____ Feed and harvest the grapevine
_____ Develop meeting skills and behavior (see p. 127)
_____ Bear bad news sensitively
_____ Use specific communication skills when hiring and interviewing
_____ Negotiate carefully (see p. 105)
_____ Navigate through a conflict or disagreement
_____ Remove yourself if you are about to lose control
_____ Always be tactful

SELECTED BIBLIOGRAPHY

Carter, Nancy Carol. "Communication as a Tool of Organizational Renewal in Law Libraries." _Law Library Journal_ 81 (Spring 1989): 221–39.

Green, Thad B., and Jay T. Knippen. _Breaking the Barrier to Upward Communication: Strategies and Skills for Employees, Managers and HR Specialists._ Westport, Conn.: Quorum Bks., 1999.

Griffin, Jack. _How to Say It at Work._ Paramus, N.J.: Prentice Hall, 1998.

Hanna, Michael S., and Gerald L. Wilson. _Communicating in Business and Professional Settings._ 4th ed. New York: Random House, 1998.

Longenecker, Clinton O., and Jack L. Simonetti. _Getting Results: Five Absolutes for High Performance._ San Francisco, Calif.: Jossey-Bass, 2001.

Lubans, John. "'While I Was Busy Holding On, You Were Busy Letting Go': Reflections on E-mail Networks and the Demise of Hierarchical Communication." _Library Administration & Management_ 14, no. 1 (Winter 2000): 18–21.

Reed, Peter J. _Extraordinary Leadership._ London: Kogan-Page, 2001.

Notes

Interdepartmental Relations

ANDREA KAPPLER
Cataloging Manager
Evansville Vanderburgh Public Library

Technical services managers of all levels must nurture positive relationships in two key areas. The first is within the department. Maintaining communications among collection development, acquisitions, cataloging, serials, bindery, etc. is vital to running an efficient technical services operation. Not knowing what is going on in technical services is all too easy, even when it is a small operation.

The other area to develop and maintain positive relationships is with other departments within an organization. These areas can include the library or campus administration, the information technology department, and public services. Nurturing these relationships is more important than ever in light of tighter budgets and the outsourcing movement. Quite often, technical services departments must prove their worth to their organizations by producing more with fewer staff while efficiently using complex new technologies, such as Web or Java-based integrated library systems (ILS). Yet many administrators, information technology staffs, and public services librarians think of technical services as a backroom operation that is optional to the overall function of a library.

Therefore, the challenge for you is to develop an effective communication model that can close the gaps among these departments, both internal and external. A technical services department that runs efficiently based on good relationships between internal departments can make a favorable impression on those in external departments, such as the administration.

I. **Division heads, department heads, and branch managers**
    _____ Find out who they are and introduce yourself to them
    _____ Know who manages specific collections
    _____ Know who supervises library assistants, clerks, shelvers, pages, and others
    _____ Know who manages the computer or information technology (IT) department
    _____ Ask them their preferred form of communication (e-mail, phone, etc.)
    _____ Ask them to invite you to their meetings when necessary
    _____ Invite them to technical services for a tour
    _____ Invite them to technical services for a meeting when necessary

II. **Technical services staff**

_____ Provide other library staff with a list of names, e-mail, and phone numbers for technical services staff

_____ Include on this list whom to contact for problems or questions in areas such as collection development, ordering, bindery, classification problems, etc.

_____ Keep the list up-to-date when staff changes, and redistribute it

III. **Public services work**

_____ Work in public services periodically

_____ Ask public services staff for input on issues such as labels, collections, binding schedules, or end processing of library materials

_____ Thank public services staff for their input when solving problems, making policy, or procedure changes

IV. **Technical services procedures and policies**

_____ Make technical services' policies and procedures easily available to all departments

_____ Develop a procedure for handling materials needing corrections, repairs, etc.

   _____ Incorrect labels

   _____ Incorrect item locations in the OPAC

   _____ Incorrect or missing barcodes

   _____ Problems with an assigned class number

_____ Provide a format for reporting errors

   _____ E-mail

   _____ Paper printout

   _____ Phone call

   _____ Special form on library Web site or staff Intranet page

_____ Inform public services staff in advance when classification schemes face major changes

_____ Develop policies specifying whether older materials will be reclassified or if changed classification areas will be weeded

_____ Inform public services staff when OPAC indexing changes or enhancements or other changes are made to the local ILS system

_____ Inform public services staff when different types of MARC records are added to the OPAC for unusual materials, such as electronic books, Web sites, or other special formats

SELECTED BIBLIOGRAPHY

Intner, Sheila S. *Interfaces: Relationships between Library Technical and Public Services.* Englewood, Colo.: Libraries Unlimited, 1993.

Negotiation

EMILY BERGMAN
Head of Collections and Technical Services
Occidental College

MARLENE SLOUGH
Head of Acquisitions
Eastern Illinois University

Negotiating is a way of life for managers. People disagree, they have conflicts of interests, and you, the manager, will need to negotiate to find a form of joint action that seems better to each stakeholder than the alternatives. Negotiators must manage the inescapable tension between cooperative moves to create value for all and competitive moves to claim value for each. Interdependence, some perceived conflict, opportunistic potential, and the possibility of agreement are four of the key elements of negotiation that widely occur. Inspecting a management situation and finding these four elements should suggest strongly the possibility of negotiation. More precisely, negotiation can be characterized as a process of potentially opportunistic interaction by which two or more parties, with some apparent conflict, seek to do better through jointly decided action than they could otherwise.

An agreement may range in form from a legal document to an implicit understanding. Quite often, agreements do not formally bind the parties, or not for long. Revision of contracts and understandings is almost as common as the negotiation that led to them in the first place. Negotiation may be acknowledged and explicit or unacknowledged and tacit. The basis for agreement may be a conventional quid pro quo, or it may include actions that further identical interests but that do not involve a material exchange.

You will find yourself in all kinds of situations that require this process and closely related activities that are amenable to similar analysis (mediation, arbitration, changing the game, influencing decisions at some remove). Negotiation must encompass more than parties formally exchanging offers to fashion a quid pro quo. It must allow for the subtlety of interests in shared purposes and intense concern with process as well as more tangible stakes. It must incorporate a shifting mix of cooperative and competitive elements and admit moves to change the game itself. It should be systematic and adapted to managerial considerations.

I. Planning and preparation

A. Collect the necessary information

1. About yourself

    ____ Your goals

    ____ Your specific objectives

    ____ Your needs and the outcomes that would satisfy you

    ____ The tradeoffs or compromises you are willing to consider

    ____ What you are willing to risk

    ____ Whether you are willing to take risks in the negotiation

    ____ Alternatives if you fail to reach agreement

    ____ The amount of leverage or power you have

    ____ How you are perceived by the other party

    ____ Your deadlines

2. About the other party

    ____ Their goals

    ____ Their specific objectives

    ____ Their power to come to an agreement, make decisions, and make them stick

    ____ The right person with whom to negotiate

    ____ What they are willing to risk

    ____ Their alternatives if they fail to reach agreement

    ____ Their styles

    ____ Their deadlines

3. About the topic or issue

    ____ What is usually done

    ____ Whether or when exceptions to the rule are made

    ____ What objective standards or guidelines exist for judging this situation

    ____ What the reasonable standards are on which both parties can agree

B. Before you begin negotiation

    ____ Build a good, trusting relationship with the other party

    ____ Gain support from others who can strengthen your case and go to bat for you

    ____ Identify barriers and obstacles

II. Negotiation session

A. Let the other party know

    ____ That you have power and are a decision-maker

    ____ That you will listen carefully to everything the other party has to offer

    ____ That you respect the other party's position

    ____ What exactly needs to be accomplished

B. During negotiation

    ____ Keep everyone on the issues

    ____ Avoid attacks, no matter the provocation

    ____ Stay rational

    ____ Avoid bluffing

    ____ Listen carefully

    ____ Avoid being pressured by negotiating tactics

    ____ Look for alternatives

    ____ Actively engage everyone in problem-solving discussions

    ____ Have support that gives the other negotiator a rationale for agreeing with you

    ____ State and clarify the agreement and be sure everyone agrees on the decision

III. **Negotiation in a unionized environment**
  A. Know and understand the union contract and its implications for your unit
    ____ Compensation
    ____ Hiring
    ____ Promotion
    ____ Job classification
    ____ Retention
    ____ Grievance procedures
    ____ Training
    ____ Governance
    ____ Benefits
  B. Become acquainted with available support personnel
    ____ Legal counsel
    ____ Library personnel officer
    ____ Human resources personnel
    ____ Union steward
    ____ Union delegates
    ____ Union negotiators

IV. **Negotiating with vendors for products and services**
  A. Determine the negotiation party
    ____ Library representative (dean, director, unit head, librarian, etc.)
    ____ Campus representative (director of purchasing, legal counsel, etc.)
    ____ Consortial representatives (statewide, regional, local, etc.)
  B. Be aware of negotiation protocols
    ____ Local and state government guidelines
    ____ Local and state government procurement regulations
    ____ Signature authority
    ____ Request for proposal (RFP) requirement
  C. Educate yourself about your library to determine the services and products required or desired
    ____ User surveys
    ____ Staff surveys
    ____ Focus groups
    ____ Analysis of library assessment data and statistics
    ____ Technology requirements and limitations of your library
  D. Educate yourself about the vendor and the vendor's competitors
    ____ Consider technology requirements and limitations of the products
    ____ Request a list of current clients with contact information
    ____ Ask for an in-house demonstration
    ____ Ask for a product trial
    ____ Determine customer support
    ____ Evaluate product documentation
    ____ Determine availability of reporting and statistics
    ____ Determine whether products meet the library's minimum specifications
    ____ Ask the vendor to agree in writing to prices, modules, service, or special programming

V. **Negotiating salary**
  A. Before the interview, articulate what is most important to you and differentiate between what you want and what you need
    ____ Money

    ____ Flexible schedule

    ____ Professional development opportunities

    ____ Benefits (leave, medical, dental, etc.)

    ____ Opportunity for advancement

    ____ Other

B. At the interview, be prepared to articulate your strengths

    ____ Work experience

    ____ Education

    ____ Specialized training

    ____ Natural talent

    ____ Other

C. Maintain dialog throughout the process

    ____ Be firm

    ____ Be flexible

    ____ Be receptive to unanticipated possibilities

SELECTED BIBLIOGRAPHY

ACRL Status of Academic Librarians Committee. "Faculty Status and Collective Bargaining Statements: Final Versions." *College & Research Libraries News* 62, no. 3 (Mar. 2001): 304–306.

Coco, Carolyn. "Working with Library Vendors: Trouble-free Negotiations." *LLA Bulletin* 61, no. 3 (Winter 1998): 163–71.

Eastern Illinois University Chapter of Local 4100, University Professionals of Illinois (IFT, AFT, AFL-CIO). Example of an Academic Library Union Contract. www.eiu.edu/~EiuUpi (accessed May 3, 2007).

Kleinman, Marcia P. *Executive Negotiating Program.* New York: Thomas, 1989.

Kolb, Deborah M., and Ann C. Schaffner. "Negotiating What You're Worth." *Library Journal* 126, no. 17 (Oct. 2001): 52–53.

Lax, David A., and James K. Sebenius. *The Manager as Negotiator: Bargaining for Cooperation and Competitive Gain.* New York: The Free Pr., 1986.

Moore, Amanda. "For Immediate Results, Sign Without Thinking: Brief Comments on Negotiating Licensing Agreements." *Arkansas Libraries* 58, no. 3 (Jun. 2001): 18–20.

New York Public Library Guild, Local 1930 (AFSCME, AFL-CIO). Example of a Public Library Union Contract. www.local1930.org/contract/contract.html (accessed May 3, 2007).

Satin, Seymour. "Negotiating: From First Contact to Final Contract." *Searcher* 9, no. 6 (Jun. 2001): 50–54.

Weber, Mark. "Support Staff Unions in Academic and Public Libraries: Some Suggestions for Managers with Reference to the Ohio Experience, 1984-1990." *Journal of Library Administration* 17, no. 3 (1992): 65–86.

Networking

NANCY LEE MYERS
Acquisitions Librarian and Professor
University of South Dakota

Networking is more than just the maxim, "it's who you know." Networking brings together a group of individuals with common interests who can be of mutual assistance or who provide helpful information. A network even may be made of people who can be helpful professionally, perhaps in finding a job or moving up in an organization. In another way, however, the network, made up of contacts—and those contacts' contacts—can help you quickly find who can help you get what you need, as well as helping others do the same. Those personal and professional contacts might be useful not only for referrals, advice, and information, but also just for support. Those networking relationships are maintained through reciprocal communication. The effort of developing nourishing networks is definitely a part of the success of a new manager.

I. **Key people to include in your network**
   A. Formal networks in your library
      _____ Supervisor
      _____ Your supervisor's supervisor
      _____ Your subordinates
      _____ Key decision-making committees
      _____ Your peers in other departments or units
   B. Informal networks in your library
      _____ Think about who always hears the latest news on the grapevine. According to Raye-Johnson, "The grapevine has an accuracy rate of more than 75 percent."[1]
      _____ Those who make decisions beyond their authority
      _____ Those who often find people asking them for advice
   C. Networks outside your library
      _____ Board or advisory group that makes policy for your library
      _____ Local, state, regional, or national professional organizations

1. Venda Raye-Johnson, *Effective Networking: Proven Techniques for Career Success* (Menlo Park, Calif.: Crisp, 1990),

_____ Organizations in your school, university, town, or business that might have an impact on your library

_____ Potential donors or granting agencies

II. Goals in networking

_____ Get accurate, up-to-date information in a rapidly changing organizational climate

_____ Find people to go to for advice in responding to a crisis or for planning for the future

_____ Find people to support you in working to reach your goals

_____ Find people you would like to assist in achieving their potential

_____ Find people who can help you get a transfer, a promotion, or a different job

_____ Find people who have specialized knowledge to help you increase your skills and expertise

_____ Find people who know people who can help

III. Effective networking

_____ Introduce yourself to strangers

_____ Meet people you know who can be helpful to you

_____ Ask for advice

_____ Be a good listener

_____ Offer help when you are able

_____ Share information and skills when they will benefit others

_____ Find appropriate mentors for yourself

_____ Serve as a role model or mentor for someone else

_____ Use meetings, conferences, and social events to increase your network

_____ Make yourself visible by participating in organizations

_____ Maintain a Rolodex of business cards and contact information

SELECTED BIBLIOGRAPHY

Boe, Anne. *NetWorking Success: How to Turn Business & Financial Relationships into Fun & Profit.* Deerfield Beach, Fla.: Health Communications, 1994.

Hadley, Joyce, and Betsy Sheldon. *The Smart Woman's Guide to Networking.* Franklin Lakes, N.J.: Career Pr., 1995.

MacKay, Harvey. *Dig Your Well Before You're Thirsty: The Only Networking Book You'll Ever Need.* New York: Currency/ Doubleday, 1997.

Raye-Johnson, Venda. *Effective Networking: Proven Techniques for Career Success.* Menlo Park, Calif.: Crisp, 1990.

Time Management

Time Management Tools and Tips

STEPHEN COCHRAN

Librarian

Washington State Department of Transportation

First time managers are often astounded at how busy they are! The lyrics of Gershwin's "Fascinatin' Rhythm" come to mind:

Each morning I get up with the Sun—
always hopping, never stopping—
to find at night no work has been done.

Certainly, most new managers have found themselves wondering how the workday managed to get so much shorter so quickly. The truth of the matter is time cannot be managed. "You manage activities, not time."[1] Finding ways to make the most of your time is essential to your success as a manager.

"To talk about time as being organized or managed is a misnomer. Time is already organized. It is counted in precisely the same orderly increments the world over. You can, however, manage your own use of time. Learn to use the clock as a tool."[2]

The remainder of this chapter outlines some ideas about time and then presents you with a checklist of considerations about how effectively you fit your activities into your schedule.

MANAGING ACTIVITIES

Vilfredo Pareto (1848–1923) was an Italian economist who estimated that 80 percent of the most important work we do is accomplished in 20 percent of the available time; conversely, the remaining 20 percent of the less important work eats up the remaining 80 percent of time. This 80/20 rule is known as the Pareto Principle.

1. Judith A. Siess, *Time Management, Planning, and Prioritization for Librarians* (Lanham, Md.: Scarecrow Pr., 2002), 3.
2. Anne Marie Turner, "Organizing from the Inside Out," online course, Barnes and Noble University, Sept. 2001.]

Therefore, your two top priorities should be: (1) eliminating timewasters, and (2) insuring that you delegate as much of the time-consuming 20 percent of your work that is less important to those employees whose time is less costly.

Timewasters are "activities that take up large amounts of time without corresponding value."[3] Siess divides these into eight different groups of timewasters, and notes that there are timewasters that are "internal" (over which you have control) and "external" (over which you have no control).[4]

I. Personal (all personal timewasters are internal):

_____ Do not be a perfectionist. Accomplish your work to meet your goals, not your aesthetic standards

_____ Say "no" to those delegating work to you if it is outside the purview of your job

_____ Prioritize your tasks as very important, important, and not important. Further prioritize them by date due. Many automated to-do lists allow you to make these distinctions and then rank your list for you

_____ Do not let negative emotions (such as guilt, anger, fear, etc.) or negative attitudes affect your work

_____ Organize your files, your schedule and calendar, and your to-do list

_____ Clarify for your reporting staff those jobs that are yours and the jobs you expect them to do

_____ Give those who have responsibility for performing certain jobs the authority to do the work; otherwise, they will be delayed by needing permissions from others before being able to move forward

_____ Rethink the delegation, if you end up redoing—or duplicating—any of the work you delegate

_____ Give yourself enough rest, and take relaxing breaks during your day

_____ Be a good listener, and practice listening to others for new ideas and ways of approaching the flow of work

_____ Do not try to do too much, spread yourself too thin, or waste your most productive hours of the day

_____ Minimize the amount of time you spend socializing and traveling to other offices to gossip, while allowing yourself the necessary time to form important human bonds with your fellow workers

II. Other people

_____ Do not spend any more time than you have to putting out fires. Let others, preferably the firestarters, put these out; they will be less likely to start fires in the future

_____ Do not micromanage assistants

_____ Set aside closed door times to minimize interruptions

_____ Do not organize for a disorganized boss, but give friendly reminders about work you need finished in a timely way

_____ If you work with others who procrastinate, have low morale, or who hand you their personal problems to deal with, bring this to their attention and suggest to them possible remedies

_____ Do not reward those who are chronically late by waiting for them to start meetings, projects, or other functions

3. Jack D. Ferner, *Successful Time Management: A Self-Teaching Guide*, 2nd ed. (New York: Wiley, 1995), 12.
4. Seiss, *Time Management, Planning, and Prioritization for Librarians*, 11–13.

_____ Do not sit down with salespeople who appear without an appointment. Ask them when they will next be in the area, and make a date with them. Be courteous but firm, and then show them the door

III. **Machines**

_____ Know how to operate all the equipment your job calls upon you to use and keep user guides handy

_____ Have frequently called numbers on speed dial, keep an up-to-date e-mail address book, and keep your Web sites organized in a links list associated with your browser, so that you do not have to look theses things up each time you need them

_____ Have regularly scheduled preventative maintenance performed upon the machines on which you rely to do your work

_____ Have technology that is up-to-date and useful

IV. **Methods and procedures**

_____ Have a routine workflow for all of your regularly scheduled tasks

_____ Batch things like copying, metering mail, and delivering materials to other offices

_____ Do not talk with your boss or colleagues about each step of your project. Instead, have regularly scheduled meetings where you update them on progress

_____ Have a well-written and up-to-date policy, procedure, and regulation manual

_____ Have a to-do list that is prioritized and updated on a regular—at least weekly—basis

_____ Do not involve more people than you need in a project or decision

_____ Reduce clutter in your work area

_____ Reuse what you have already done, if it is applicable; do not reinvent the wheel

_____ Have tickler files or reminder notes to keep you abreast of upcoming events

_____ Develop standards, or work objectives, against which you measure your productivity

V. **Procrastination**

_____ Do not wait until the last minute

_____ Complete tasks or communications first that you think will be unpleasant

_____ Do not wait until the so-called appropriate time to do certain work

_____ Do not just do it yourself rather than take the time to teach someone else

_____ Finish what you start; do not leave multiple things dangling

_____ Unless the work simply is not getting done, do not take back jobs that you have previously delegated

_____ "Estimate long and deliver short" in your estimations of how long a project will take

VI. **Management**

_____ Do not micromanage others or allow yourself to be micromanaged by your boss

_____ Do not overly involve yourself in the details of another's work, unless it appears they do not understand the details fully or consistently, or they are doing the work incorrectly

_____ Manage conflict, do not let it manage you

_____ Do not end up sorting mail: routing things to others that should have been routed there in the first place

_____ While it is fine to request being kept in the loop, do not put yourself in the position of having to sign off on, or approve of, everything

_____ Have a clear job description, and know what you are expected to do

VII. **Planning**

_____ Develop and use a long-range or strategic plan

_____ Make a weekly or daily plan, and stick with it

_____ Do not fall victim to the paralysis of analysis: Plans should be followed by actions, or they are not worth the paper they are printed on

_____ Do not accept plans as inflexible givens; be able to change plans to meet changing demands

VIII. Communication

_____ Do not write a memo when you could talk

_____ Do not write when you should call or vice versa

_____ Communicate clearly, concisely, and courteously

_____ Answer questions in full, and always ask, "Have I answered your question adequately?"

_____ Do not use vocabulary as a weapon, and do not leave out important information

As you can see, most of the timewasters are things that you can control, and you must. Most of the things you can do to improve your use of time are simply a matter of habit: You need to get into it, and then it is easy and routine. Start today!

MANAGING PEOPLE

If you think managing projects takes time, just wait until you start managing people! Managing people, even good people, takes time; managing problem employees takes even more time, both because of the increased level of oversight required and because of the need for even greater care in the documentation of steps taken in the management of problem employees.

If making and maintaining calendars, files, and lists are the key to managing projects, the making and keeping of schedules, agendas, minutes, and memos are the keys to managing people.

I. Schedules

_____ Know what you both *need* and *want* to accomplish this month; this week; today

_____ Ensure that project team members are aware of what they need to do

_____ Be sure timelines for the completion of various tasks are in place and understood

_____ Build flexibility into timelines so work that is completed earlier than anticipated will not leave a team member with nothing to do, and work that takes longer can have more resources allocated to it to quicken its completion

II. Memos

_____ The memo is addressed to everyone who needs to see it, and no more

_____ It is direct, not wordy, and to the point

_____ It can be an informational or disciplinary memo, or it can serve to document and recapitulate a conversation. Try not to write a memo that is a combination of these things

_____ If it is informational, it should convey all the needed information succinctly

_____ If it serves to recapitulate a conversation in writing, it should reflect all perspectives presented during the conversation, and it should do so clearly

_____ If you expect an action, a change in behavior, or a change in procedure to result from this memo, it should be stated explicitly and unambiguously in the memo

SELECTED BIBLIOGRAPHY

Ferner, Jack D. *Successful Time Management: A Self-Teaching Guide*. 2nd ed. New York: Wiley, 1995.

Lockwood, Georgene Muller. *The Complete Idiot's Guide to Organizing Your Life*. 4th ed. Indianapolis, Ind.: Alpha Bks., 2005.

Mayer, Jeffrey J. *Time Management for Dummies.* 2nd ed. Foster City, Calif.: IDG Bks. Worldwide, 1999.

Nelson, Bob. *Please Don't Just Do What I Tell You, Do What Needs To Be Done! Every Employee's Guide to Making Work More Rewarding.* New York: Hyperion, 2001.

Peterson, Pipi Campbell, with Mary Campbell. *Ready, Set, Organize!: A Workbook for the Organizationally Challenged.* 2nd ed. Indianapolis, Ind.: Park Avenue, 2002.

Pollar, Odette. *Organizing Your Work Space: A Guide to Personal Productivity.* Rev. ed. Menlo Park, Calif.: Crisp, 1999.

Siess, Judith A. *Time Management, Planning, and Prioritization for Librarians.* Lanham, Md.: Scarecrow Pr., 2002.

Turner, Anne Marie. "Organizing from the Inside Out." Online Course, Barnes and Noble University, Sept. 2002.

Notes

Managing Workflow

ANDREA KAPPLER
Cataloging Manager
Evansville Vanderburgh Public Library

In a technical services department, you must deal with workflow issues on a daily basis. A technical services department is much like a factory production line, with a customer (e.g., other library departments) receiving the product when it is finished. Every day new materials are received; they must be cataloged and physically processed, then sent to other departments or buildings in a timely manner. Technical services staffing and materials flow must constantly be monitored and adjusted, so that one or more areas do not become backlogged or short-changed in their workload. Whether you manage the entire department or supervise a smaller area such as acquisitions or cataloging, you must be aware of how everything from staff training to mail delivery affects the workflow.

I. **Know how departmental units are organized and staffed (whatever is appropriate to your technical services department)**
    ____ Collection development
    ____ Acquisitions
        ____ Monographs
        ____ Periodicals
    ____ Cataloging
        ____ Monographs cataloging
        ____ Serials cataloging
        ____ Nonbook formats cataloging (audiovisual, software, Web sites, digital media)
        ____ Original cataloging
        ____ Copy cataloging
    ____ Physical processing
        ____ Bindery
        ____ Preservation
    ____ Systems
    ____ Messenger/Courier service
    ____ Access Services
        ____ Circulation
        ____ Interlibrary loan

_____ Other units in your department

II. Staffing

_____ Make sure employees are trained to do their jobs and can work with minimal supervision

_____ Know employees' strengths and weaknesses so that job duties can be assigned to the most capable individuals

_____ Cross-train staff, so that more than one employee can do all or part of another employee's job

_____ Watch for excessive absenteeism and mentor problem employees

_____ If a backlog develops with one employee, provide counseling, then follow up to monitor progress

_____ Schedule employees so that during vacations and holidays, all areas of the department are sufficiently staffed

_____ Hire temporary or student workers, or use volunteers to cover staff shortages or help with backlogs

_____ Consider outsourcing cataloging and processing for:

    _____ Large donations

    _____ Special types of materials, such as foreign language materials

    _____ Easy cataloging, such as books with LC copy

III. Materials and processes

_____ Make sure the collection development and acquisitions staff place orders on a daily basis, so that no cataloging shortages or backlogs develop

_____ Regularly assess acquisitions, cataloging, and processing procedures. Streamline when and where possible

_____ Check with vendors to see if they provide physical processing (e.g., spine labels, ownership stamps, security tags)

_____ Identify materials needing priority processing as soon as possible and quickly move them through the department

_____ Make sure newly processed materials leave the department as soon as possible

_____ Make sure employees have equipment and supplies needed to do their work

_____ Make sure supplies of barcodes, labels, printer ink, etc. are sufficient and do not run out

_____ Be aware of how holidays affect the delivery of materials into and out of the department

_____ When considering whether or not to catalog new formats such as DVDs, MP3s, Web sites, or other future formats, first research the acquisition, cataloging, and physical processing needs of such materials

IV. Finance and budget

_____ Familiarize yourself with the fiscal year and monitor the materials budget so that money is spent in an appropriate time frame

_____ Work with collection development and acquisitions staff so that you are aware of monetary donations, such as gifts or grants, that may affect the departmental workflow

_____ If the materials budget increases or decreases more than 5 percent, consider adding or cross-training employees

SELECTED BIBLIOGRAPHY

Cargill, Jennifer, ed. *Library Management and Technical Services: The Changing Role of Technical Services in Library Organizations.* Binghamton, N.Y.: Haworth Pr., 1988.

Gorman, Michael. *Technical Services Today and Tomorrow.* 2nd ed. Englewood, Colo.: Libraries Unlimited, 1998.

Hirshon, Arnold, and Barbara Winters. *Outsourcing Library Technical Services: A How-To-Do-It Manual for Librarians.* New York: Neal-Schuman, 1996.

Intner, Sheila S., and Jean Weihs. *Standard Cataloging for School and Public Libraries.* 3rd ed. Englewood, Colo.: Libraries Unlimited, 2001.

Kascus, Marie A., and Dale Hale, eds. *Outsourcing Cataloging, Authority Work, and Physical Processing: A Checklist of Considerations.* Chicago: ALA, 1995.

Racine, Drew, ed. *Managing Technical Services in the 90's.* New York: Haworth Pr., 1991.

Notes

Setting Priorities

ALTHEA ASCHMAN
Head of Cataloging
Virginia Tech University

Without a clear set of priorities, library personnel lack direction for identifying their most critical tasks; this has the potential to create a reactive environment, where people jump in response to every new thing that comes before them, rather than assessing tasks or projects for their strategic merit. A clear sense of why the department is doing what it is doing and of a desired outcome enables you to identify the department's critical functions or core business. With clearly articulated priorities, the whole department can select and focus intelligently on the most important work. There will never be enough time to do everything. Remembering that not all priorities are number one is important, so learn discernment to distinguish between what is important, less important, nice to do, and unnecessary.

I. **Departmental priorities**
   - ____ Invest the necessary time in planning (see Planning section in this book, page 3)
   - ____ Develop a long-term perspective
   - ____ Know your core business or primary functions
   - ____ Set goals and objectives
   - ____ Assess goals and objectives for strategic fit with the library's overall strategic plan, goals, objectives, and mission
   - ____ Consider what actually can be accomplished taking available resources (financial, human, technology, etc.) into account
   - ____ Decide what to do now and what to postpone
   - ____ Align priorities with goals and objectives
   - ____ Communicate clearly the departmental mission, vision, goals, and objectives to the staff

II. **Personal priorities**
   - ____ Spend fifteen minutes each day planning the next day's activities, being sure to align tasks with desired accomplishments
   - ____ Overcome procrastination, decide what you are going to do (see "Decision-Making," in the Art of Management section, page 83, for help in this area), and just do it

_____ Find a planning and scheduling method that works for you
_____ Start by making a master list of all the tasks before you
_____ Select three or four that you deem most important (irrespective of the time it takes)
_____ Focus on these tasks before going on to anything else
_____ Align what you do and what you ask others to do with departmental goals
_____ Assess the overall strategic fit of your goals
_____ Rely on your ability to make wise choices
_____ Focus single-mindedly on one thing at a time
_____ Do the tasks with the highest long-term payoffs first

III. Methods for setting priorities
A. The team approach
_____ Form a team or committee to identify the priorities and make recommendations for accomplishing them
_____ Inform the team about any constraints, as this method only works when management is willing to accept the team's recommendations and find the resources to support them
_____ Have the team start by listing all the departments' tasks
_____ Have the group look at the list and decide which task they would do if they could do only one. Then, do the same for two tasks and only two tasks, and so on until each task on the list is ranked. The sequence may change when two or more tasks are integrally linked

B. The A-B-C-D-E method
_____ List all the things you need to accomplish
_____ Place a letter in the margin that divides the tasks into the following categories:
    _____ A=Very important, must do, serious negative consequences if not done
    _____ B=Important, should do, minor negative consequences if not done
    _____ C=Nice to do, not as important as A and B, no negative consequences if not done
    _____ D=Delegate or assign to someone else who can do it instead of you. If appropriate, route work to other work groups
    _____ E=Eliminate the unimportant (but sometimes pleasant) tasks
_____ Select the two most important tasks, those things that should be done above all others, and focus on these
_____ Accept that you cannot do everything in one day
_____ Review your list daily, so you know which two or three most important tasks to tackle before undertaking anything else, with no more than eight tasks on a daily to-do list

C. Ranked priority list[1]
_____ List every task you need to do
_____ Assign a priority number
    _____ 1=Most important and urgent, should be done today
    _____ 2=Important but can be done tomorrow or next week
    _____ 3=Important but can be done next month or next year
_____ Select three ones and rank by letter: A=Vital, B=Important, C=Nice
_____ Select three twos and rank by letter
_____ Select three threes and rank by letter

---

1. Chris Widener, "A Prioritized Task List," Made for Success.com, 2002, www.madeforsuccess.com (accessed Mar. 22, 2006).

_____ Do the tasks in this order: 1a, 1b, 1c, 2a, 2b, 2c, 3a, 3b, 3c
_____ If you have two tasks of equal importance (2 1a tasks for example), just choose one and do it
   D. Quadrant method[2]
      _____ Quadrant 1—Important and urgent
         _____ Crises
         _____ Deadline driven projects
         _____ Pressing problems
         _____ Require immediate attention
      _____ Quadrant 2—Important but not urgent
         _____ Tasks with long-term benefits and consequences
         _____ Tasks that make a difference
         _____ Tasks that increase production capacity
         _____ Relationship building
         _____ Recognizing opportunities
         _____ Planning and problem prevention
      _____ Quadrant 3—Not important but urgent
         _____ Interruptions
         _____ Ringing phones
         _____ Some mail, meetings, and reports
         _____ Matters that press on people, demanding a reaction
         _____ Popular activities
      _____ Quadrant 4—Not important and not urgent
         _____ Trivia, busy work, pleasant activities
         _____ Some mail, phone calls
         _____ Time wasters
   _____ Divide your tasks into the four categories (quadrants)
   _____ Attend to Quadrant 1 activities first, then look for ways to reduce their occurrence
   _____ Quadrant 2 activities are those that produce the greatest payoffs. Strive to spend most of your time in this quadrant
   _____ Stay out of Quadrants 3 and 4
   _____ Schedule your priorities, rather than prioritizing your schedule

III. **Some thoughts to ponder**
   _____ Setting priorities enables you to juggle the many demands on your time and competing tasks
   _____ Setting priorities helps a person to achieve goals that matter, rather than being overwhelmed by all the work there is to do
   _____ When in doubt about what you should do, ask "What is the best use of my time right now?"
   _____ You can no more afford to spend major time on minor things than you can to spend minor time on major things
   _____ The Pareto Principle is "80 percent of the reward comes from 20 percent of the effort," and the key to success is identifying and isolating that valuable 20 percent
   _____ Recognizing low priority work is necessary so you can ignore it whenever possible
   _____ Connecting with your priorities enables you to spend time on what matters most

2. Stephen R. Covey, _The Seven Habits of Highly Effective People_ (New York: Simon & Schuster, 1989).

_____ Setting priorities boils down to deciding what you want to accomplish, how and when you will accomplish it, afterward deciding which among those things you are going to do now, and then staying focused on the tasks until they are done, after which you get to set priorities again

SELECTED BIBLIOGRAPHY

Atherton, Michael. "ROI [i.e. Return on Investment] is a Matter of Setting Priorities." *Darwin Online* (Jan. 2003). www.darwinmag.com/read/010103/roi.html (accessed May 3, 2007).

Covey, Stephen R. *The Seven Habits of Highly Effective People.* New York: Simon & Schuster, 1989.

Covey, Stephen R., A. Roger Merrill, and Rebecca R. Merrill. *First Things First.* New York: Simon & Schuster, 1994.

Halsey, Carol. "Prioritizing Your Day to Accomplish More." Time Management Tools (2002). www.time-management-tools.com (accessed May 3, 2007).

Kurow, Dale. "What Are Your Priorities?" Dale Kurow homepage (Mar. 22, 2006). www.dalekurow.com/articles/what_are_your_priori (accessed May 3, 2007).

Mackenzie, R. Alec. *The Time Trap.* New York: AMACOM, 1990.

Muir, Scott P. "Setting Priorities for the Library Systems Office." *Library Hi Tech* 19, no. 3 (Fall 2001): 264–274.

Smith, Hyrum W. *The Ten Natural Laws of Successful Time and Life Management: Proven Strategies for Increased Productivity and Inner Peace.* New York: Warner Bks., 1994.

Tracy, Brian. "Setting Priorities." Time Management Tools (2003). www.time-management-tools.com (accessed May 3, 2007).

Wehniainen, Mary Jo. "Ten Keys to High Productivity." Time Management Tools (2003). www.time-management-tools.com (accessed May 3, 2007).

Widener, Chris. "A Prioritized Task List." Made for Success.com (2002). www.madeforsuccess.com (accessed May 3, 2007).

Effective Meetings

ALTHEA ASCHMAN
Head of Cataloging
Virginia Tech University

Meetings typically consume 10–20 percent of the work week, so being productive is in everyone's best interest. Too many meetings erode productivity. Meetings can become regular rituals—weekly, monthly, or quarterly. Technical services managers will convene and attend meetings called by others. You can control the quantity, duration, and effectiveness of the meetings of which you are in charge.

I. **When you are in charge**
   - _____ Determine whether a meeting is really necessary
     - _____ Consider if there is a less time-consuming or equally effective way to handle the concern or topic
     - _____ Determine if you can assemble the right people to attend the meeting at the time it is scheduled
     - _____ Assess your own preparation for the meeting
   - _____ Hold meetings when:
     - _____ Information needs to be disseminated to many people at the same time
     - _____ Disseminated information can be understood better when conveyed in person with opportunity for questions and answers
     - _____ Brainstorming about information received is important or productive
     - _____ Problem solving is needed
     - _____ Group decision-making is required
     - _____ Team building or creation of group identity is desirable
   - _____ Clarify the meeting's purpose
   - _____ Define expected results, outcomes, or accomplishments from the meeting
   - _____ Build commitment for ideas
   - _____ Provide a forum for feedback and communication

II. **Reasons for not holding a meeting**
   - _____ Needed participants are not available
   - _____ Insufficient time
   - _____ Inadequate or insufficient information or data

_____ Subject is trivial

_____ Subject could be handled another way

_____ Decision has already been made

_____ Purpose or desired outcome not clear

III. Meeting problems to avoid

_____ No agenda

_____ Wrong participants or key people not present

_____ Lack of preparation

_____ Too many digressions or wandering off the topic

_____ Too many participants

_____ Lack of clear goals and objectives

_____ Destructive conflict

IV. Proactive path to effective meetings

_____ Prepare

_____ Conduct the meeting and stay focused

_____ Evaluate the meeting and list ways to improve in the future

V. Meeting purpose

_____ Determine what type of meeting it is

    _____ Information (dissemination or exchange)

    _____ Problem solving

    _____ Decision making

    _____ Feedback or soliciting input

    _____ Team building or buy-in development

    _____ Other (specify) _____

_____ Prepare an agenda for every meeting

    _____ Clearly state the meeting's purpose, time, and place

    _____ Set time limits for duration of meeting and each agenda item

    _____ Distribute to participants in advance

    _____ Communicate preparation requirements to participants in advance

    _____ List any materials that participants need to bring to the meeting on the memo informing participants of the meeting

    _____ State the desired outcome or what is to be accomplished

    _____ If you do not have time to prepare for the meeting, postpone it until you do

_____ Develop goal-oriented meeting objectives

_____ Determine what the group will accomplish before the meeting

_____ If there is a product (such as a report), clearly state what it is before the meeting

_____ Document with minutes

    _____ Keep minutes simple and just record key points

    _____ Record goals and objectives of meeting

    _____ Record action items and assignments

VI. The meeting process

_____ Start and end on time

_____ When appropriate, set ground rules

_____ Stay focused on the topic

_____ If more time is needed for discussion of an agenda item, make a conscious decision to continue the discussion or to defer it to another meeting

_____ Be aware of the group dynamics

VII. People and their roles

A. Leader

_____ Takes charge

_____ Follows the agenda

_____ Clarifies roles and establishes ground rules

_____ Determines how the meeting's objectives will be achieved

_____ Summarizes decisions, actions, and assignments

_____ Rotates the role of leader if appropriate and desired

B. Facilitator. When the roles of leader and facilitator are separated, research shows that meetings are shorter and more productive with fewer follow-up meetings required

_____ Aids functioning of large, extremely important, or potentially controversial meetings

_____ Focuses the group on the issue at hand

_____ Ensures participation by everyone

_____ Regulates conversation movement

_____ Monitors time

_____ Suggests alternatives

_____ Protects people from attack

_____ Deals with conflict and aberrant behavior

_____ Remains neutral

C. Recorder

_____ Records information accurately and double checks it

_____ Keeps track of what has been covered (see section on minutes above)

_____ Produces meeting minutes

_____ Uses a standardized template, which can be helpful

D. Participants

_____ Know the purpose of the meeting ahead of time

_____ Know why they have been invited to the meeting and ascertains what their role is

_____ Confirm attendance

_____ Are on time

_____ Follow ground rules and proper decorum

_____ Contribute

_____ Are proactive in staying on track and encouraging others to do the same

_____ Note any special knowledge or skill about the subject matter

_____ Talk to the leader if they do not feel free to express their opinions or feel in competition with others

_____ Gauge their willingness to cooperate with the group in accomplishing its goals or in arriving at a decision

_____ Gauge their faith in the decision being carried out

_____ Accept personal responsibility for decisions they help make or to which they contribute

_____ If something feels odd, address concerns to the leader (in private if appropriate)

_____ If the meeting or being on a committee feels like a waste of time, try to figure out why

_____ If they find that they neither contribute nor learn anything from the group, try to find ways to remove themselves

_____ When required to attend some meetings no matter what, do so without complaint, which is in their best interest

VIII. Behavioral problems of which to be aware

_____ Side conversations

_____ Quiet participants who say very little

____ Domineering or overly talkative participants
____ Disagreeable or disruptive participants

IX. **Ways to cope with difficult people in meetings**
____ Signal nonverbally
____ Listen actively
____ Stop side conversations by asking those participants if they have something to share with the group
____ Invoke ground rules
____ Connect on a personal level
____ Change the process or the topic
____ Ignore mildly negative behavior
____ Discuss highly negative behavior privately with involved individuals
____ Do not take things personally
____ Stop the meeting if it becomes counterproductive

X. **Place of meeting**
____ Determine what is important for the meeting setting
____ Environment: room size, seating arrangement, lighting, noise, temperature, access
____ Equipment
____ Backup plan if equipment or technology fails

XI. **Self-development**
____ Study diligently and on an ongoing basis to learn and perfect the skill set required for managing meetings
____ Read and apply all you can about group process if you preside in meetings
____ Study and master communication techniques and skills
____ Challenge yourself to operate with fewer meetings
____ Take advantage of training: workshops on effective meetings, facilitator training, assertiveness training, conflict resolution, and communication skills are very useful

ACKNOWLEDGEMENT

Most of the material for this section was taken from the workshop "How to Conduct Effective and Efficient Meetings: Tips and Techniques," by Steve Van Akin and Dick Harshberger, University Leadership Development, Virginia Tech, Blacksburg, Va. (Oct. 27, 1999, and Sept. 25–26, 2001).

HELPFUL WEB SITES

EffectiveMeetings.com. www.effectivemeetings.com (accessed May 3, 2007).
MeetingWizard.org. www.meetingwizard.org (accessed May 3, 2007). Click on "Effective Meetings" or other topic of interest.
McNamara, Carter. "Basic Guide to Conducting Effective Meetings." www.mapnp.org/library/misc/mtgmgmnt.htm (accessed May 3, 2007).

SELECTED BIBLIOGRAPHY

Dunsing, Richard J. *You and I Have Got to Stop Meeting This Way: How to Run Better Meetings in Business and Industry.* New enlarged ed. New York: AMACOM, 1981.
McCallister, Linda. *I Wish I'd Said That: How to Talk Yourself Out of Trouble and Into Success.* New York: Wiley, 1992.
Streibel, Barbara J. *The Manager's Guide to Effective Meetings.* New York: McGraw-Hill, 2003.
Timm, Paul R. *How to Hold Successful Meetings: 30 Action Tips for Managing Effective Meetings.* Franklin Lakes, N.J.: Career Pr., 1997.

Notes

Notes

Printed in the United States
78895LV00006B/265-436

9 780838 984130